Preparing to Teach God's Word

G. Raymond Carlson

Gospel Publishing House • **Springfield, Missouri**

02-0579

PREPARING TO TEACH GOD'S WORD
© 1975 by the Gospel Publishing House
Springfield, Missouri 65802
All Rights Reserved

Library of Congress Catalog Card Number: 75-5221

This is a Workers Training Division
textbook. Credit for its study will be issued
under Classification 2, Sunday School Department,
Assemblies of God.

Printed in the United States of America

Contents

1

The Bible Is for You

Do YOU FIND THE BIBLE hard to understand? Do you read your Bible on the basis of a "have-to" approach? Are you tempted to bypass Bible reading because you don't get anything out of it? Is your time with the Bible like a long forced march across a hot, barren desert with only an occasional stop for a cool drink and refreshing rest?

Too many Christians find Bible reading a drudgery. For some the Bible is a flower or leaf press, a catchall for clippings, a place to record the family tree, or a place to keep a favorite picture.

The Bible has been a forbidden Book to some people in Christendom. We Protestants have always felt that the Bible was to be read by our members, and perhaps we have felt rather smug and even self-righteous regarding our stance. But now we see the Roman church turning to our position. They openly encourage their members to buy and read the Scriptures, including in some instances the Protestant translations. But what is happening among Protestants? Where the Romanists used to have a forbidden Book, the Protestants seem to have a forbidding Book. Possibly ecclesiastical jargon has frightened some people as men talk of the "original Greek," the context, and high-sounding terms of theology.

To whom did God write His Word? It is for everyone, not just for "professionals." Let people begin to study the Bible, personally, in classes and in services. And let people study the

Bible itself. For too long the emphasis has been on books about the Bible rather than on the Bible itself. Believers need to be encouraged in daily searching—digging, pondering, praying. Give instruction in the principles of interpretation, historical background, and other essentials for the proper handling of the Word, and then get the Bible to the people and people to the Bible.

When people become involved in Bible study the recruitment of Sunday school teachers will not be as difficult. Parents will instruct their children in God's Word, the young will become conversant with the reasons for their faith, and the church will stabilize in spiritual maturity.

You Can Enjoy the Bible

Are Christians supposed to enjoy the Bible? What does the Bible say about its ability to produce joy? The Psalmist testifies, "Thy testimonies have I taken as a heritage for ever: for they are the rejoicing of my heart" (Psalm 119:111).

The prophet Jeremiah states, "Thy words were found, and I did eat them; and thy word was unto me the joy and rejoicing of mine heart" (Jeremiah 15:16).

Jesus himself gives us a two-fold purpose for His spoken words: "These things have I spoken unto you, that my joy might remain in you, and that your joy might be full" (John 15:11).

When we enjoy the Bible we will turn to it daily for spiritual food. There is no possibility of living a victorious Christian life unless we come to the Bible repeatedly and meaningfully.

Three Secrets

In Bible reading there are three secrets to enjoyment: (1) the secret of appreciation, (2) the secret of understanding, and (3) the secret of participation. These factors contribute to the enjoyment of all facets of life. Let the following illustrate:

Watch a musician perform. Many enjoy his music, but only those with an appreciation of the difficulties of performance, the discipline of study and practice, and the use of technique enjoy it to the fullest.

Listen to two men describe a "ham" radio operation. They use terms meaningless to the uninformed and enjoy discussing their hobby because of mutual understanding.

Fishing catches the attention of millions. One might try this sport; but, if he never caught a fish, his interest would lessen. Let him catch a "big" one, and he could well become a confirmed fisherman. He has experienced participation.

SECRET OF APPRECIATION

To enjoy the Bible there must be an appreciation of it as the Word of God—its background, its value, its power. The Bible is a unique Book, making claims for itself and using expressions found nowhere else in all literature. More than a good book, it is the inspired, authoritative, infallible, inerrant Word of Almighty God. Despite its diverse authorship and content, the Bible shows an amazing unity of design and purpose, for it has a single theme—redemption. There never has been such a book as the Bible because there never has been such a message. There has never been such a message, for there has never been such a person as Christ. The message is not a code of ethics but a way of life. No one can live up to its standards in his own strength. This is only possible through the transforming power of the seed of the Word bearing life in our hearts by the regenerating work of the Holy Spirit. And that same Holy Spirit is given by God to us to be our Guide in the reading, study, and enjoyment of the Bible.

SECRET OF UNDERSTANDING

To enjoy reading the Bible one must read with understanding. The Bible is an open Book available to all, but to a vast number it is a closed Book because they do not approach it in a manner to understand it. To understand the Bible is to enjoy it. Understanding comes by a definite commitment of faith and by submission to the Holy Spirit. We can read and study without profit unless we exercise faith in the truths read. Often we could be charged, "O . . . slow of heart to believe" (Luke 24:25). When we open our hearts by faith the Spirit of God takes over.

The impenitent heart will find the Bible but a skeleton of facts without flesh or life or breath. Shakespeare may be enjoyed without penitence; we may understand Plato without believing a word he says; but penitence, humility, faith, and obedience are needed for us to understand God's Word. The natural man must know in order to believe; the spiritual man must believe in order to know. The Bible is a supernatural Book and can be understood only by supernatural aid.

But there are Christians who have difficulty understanding the Bible. What about their problem? Testimony to the difficulties encountered is too full and too widespread to be dismissed lightly. This will be dealt with at length as consideration is given to the various approaches to systematic, creative study of the Word of God.

SECRET OF PARTICIPATION

To enjoy the Bible is to read and study with participation. Ask yourself, "How does this affect me, my life, my faith, my experience, my walk, my service?" Apply the truths to your own life. "Do I have faith like Abraham, meekness like Moses, singleness of purpose like Daniel, a heart after God like David, goodness like Barnabas, power like Paul?"

To enjoy the Bible, approach it with appreciation as the Word of God, with understanding through prayerful study, and with willing participation in applying its message in personal living.

F. B. Meyer said in a picturesque manner:

Read the Bible, not as a newpaper, but as a home letter. If a cluster of heavenly fruit hangs within reach, gather it. If a promise lies upon the page as a blank check, cash it. If a prayer is recorded, appropriate it, and launch it as a feathered arrow from the bow of your desire. If an example of holiness gleams before you, ask God to do as much for you. If the truth is revealed in all its intrinsic splendor, entreat that its brilliance may ever irradiate the hemisphere of your life.

Spiritual Success

Spiritual success for both an individual and a church can come only through study and meditation on the Word of God. A greater use and understanding of the Bible by believers is essential to a living, dynamic church. D. L. Moody said, "I never saw a useful Christian who was not a student of the Bible. If a man neglects his Bible, he may pray and ask God to use him in his work, but God cannot make much use of him for there is not much for the Holy Spirit to work upon. We must have the Word itself, which is sharper than any two-edged sword."

Many Christians do not get that extra something—joy and satisfaction—from their Bible study. They have failed to learn how to make studying the Word a feeding process that results in spiritual nourishment and growth. Most Christians read a portion of the Bible each day as a devotional exercise. This is good; it is necessary and profitable. But too many believers follow the practice of reading Bible portions; they never read the Scriptures in any other way.

System is Needed

Systematic study of the Bible is needful. A knowledge of the Bible, or any one book of the Bible, comes by a definite plan of reading and studying. Reading portions will feed the soul, but a Christian needs to grasp and understand the great truths and doctrines which the Bible teaches. Bible study must not be an end in itself. God has given His Word to us, and it is to do something in us and through us. It deserves our devoted, systematic study.

You Can Understand the Bible

The Bible was given for man to understand the will of God and not to veil the will of God. The right understanding of the Scriptures has always been a challenge to the Church. Response to this challenge is open to constant risk because any human attempt to understand the Word of God also opens the door to the possibility of misunderstanding. This is illustrated in the Scriptures themselves. For instance, the Pharisees distorted the law. Church history records the many battles that have raged over an understanding of the Bible. There was the Christological controversy in the early history of the Church, the controversy between Augustine and Pelagius, the conflict of Luther and Calvin with Rome, the conflict of Calvinism and Arminianism.

The traditions and dogmas set forth by men must be tested with the Word of God. If the Reformers had contented themselves with tradition, we would never have known the blessings of the Reformation. Rome accused the Reformers of breaking with tradition and of setting aside the Holy Spirit's guidance of the Church. The Reformers rejected that judgment; they only wanted to test the position against the Word. It was a matter of priorities. The authority of the Church is not final; the final authority is the Word of God. Tradition that cannot stand up under the light of revelation must be put aside. And some traditions draw a veil of misunderstanding over crucial portions of Holy Scripture.

STUDY TAKES DISCIPLINE

Personal Bible study is a battle. The study of the Word is the most effective tool of the Holy Spirit to bring Christians into conformity to Christ. Understandably, Satan uses every device possible to keep us from the Word of God. If our personal Bible study is to open the will of God for our lives, we will need to apply ourselves to the task. To accomplish our purpose there will be a need for certain methods that are governed by some basic rules. If we will heed the admonition and follow the rules laid down in Proverbs 2:1-4, we can expect the results outlined in verse 5: "My son, if thou wilt receive my words, and hide my commandments with thee; so that thou incline thine ear unto wisdom, and apply thine heart to understanding; yea, if thou criest after knowledge, and liftest up thy voice for understanding; if thou seekest her as silver, and searchest for her as for hid treasures; then shalt thou understand the fear of the Lord, and find the knowledge of God" (Proverbs 2:1-5).

Rules to Follow

1. *The Bible is God's Word.* "My son, if thou wilt receive my words." We must come to the Bible with the conviction that it is the Word of God through which God will surely speak to us. We do not need to prove the Bible first and then accept it; we accept it and then let it prove itself. If we doubt the authority of the Word, we cannot expect to receive anything from the Lord (James 1:6, 7). We need to be like the Thessalonians and receive "the word of God . . . as truth" (1 Thessalonians 2:13). Many receive no benefit because they do not receive the Word with faith (Hebrews 4:2).

2. *Obedience is required.* "Hide my commandments with thee." The soul must be exercised by the Word. It must school us and change our lives. If we fail to translate the Word into daily practice we will be spiritually anemic. Bible study brings renewed devotion to God. Even more, it produces discipline and determination resulting in the transformation of human nature. There is no better way to blind ourselves to Bible truth than to refuse to heed and obey it. Hosea the prophet said, "My people are destroyed for lack of knowledge: because thou hast rejected knowledge, I will also reject thee" (Hosea 4:6). We do not truly study the Word, we do not really know it until we put it into practice in our lives. "Be ye doers of the Word" (James 1:22-25).

3. *Listening is demanded.* "Incline thine ear unto wisdom." The word *incline* means to "listen," to "take heed." Luke (8:18) says, "Take heed therefore how ye hear." We need to incline our ears to the voice of the Holy Spirit. A first step in Bible study is to learn to read intelligently. But more than that, we need the illumination of the Holy Spirit, for the Bible is a revelation of spiritual truth, and its understanding is dependent upon spiritual sensitivity. Consider every phrase, every word of Scripture. Let the Holy Spirit make it real to the listening ear.

4. *The heart must be yielded.* "Apply thine heart to understanding." Heart-searching should precede Bible study. The Word has been likened in Scripture to seed. We must prepare

the soil of our hearts to receive the Word so that it will bear fruit. The Psalmist prayed, "Search me, O God, and know my heart: try me, and know my thoughts: and see if there be any wicked way in me" (Psalm 139:23, 24). Unless the heart is prepared, we will miss the truths of the Word. We must have a regenerated heart (John 3:3), a humble heart (Matthew 11:25), a willing heart (John 7:17), and a devoted heart (Psalm 119:97). We need to open our hearts to God and let Him prepare them to receive the truth of His Word.

5. *Prayer is necessary.* "Yea, if thou criest after knowledge, and liftest up thy voice for understanding." We cannot, by our wisdom, understand the Bible. In all our study we must carefully seek the help of the Holy Spirit. He alone can remove the veil from our minds. It is impossible to know the Bible without prayer. We need to join the Psalmist in his prayer, "Open thou mine eyes, that I may behold wondrous things out of thy law" (Psalm 119:18). When we breathe this prayer in faith, we can expect the Lord to open our understanding as He did for the disciples after His resurrection and for Lydia, the seller of purple. "Then opened he their understanding, that they might understand the Scriptures" (Luke 24:45). "And a certain woman named Lydia ... whose heart the Lord opened" (Acts 16:14).

6. *Seek as for silver.* "If thou seekest her as silver." Silver is a standard of money. Men will do almost anything for money because money gives them so many of the things they want. The Bible states, "money answereth all things" (Ecclesiastes 10:19). Men work for the paycheck. But there is something of far greater worth than the silver of this world. David said, "The words of the Lord are pure words: as silver tried in a furnace of earth, purified seven times" (Psalm 12:6). As a man disciplines himself to hard toil to get a share of this world's goods, the Christian must prepare for the discipline of businesslike prayer. It takes earnestness of purpose, concentration of effort, and determination of mind and heart.

7. *Search as for hidden treasure.* "Searchest for her as for hid treasures." The word *searchest* is equivalent to "dig." One

translation (Vulgate) reads "to dig out." The treasures of God's Word are to be found by the one who will give himself to diligently dig for them. We need to use the same untiring energy with which men dig for hidden treasure in our search for the riches of the Word. The perseverance of the seeker after material wealth often puts to shame the seeker after spiritual wealth. To search is important. Jesus said, "Search the Scriptures" (John 5:39).

RESULTS TO EXPECT

1. *Understanding.* "Then shalt thou understand the fear of the Lord." Our hearts will be filled with wonder and praise, and we will receive "the things of the Spirit of God" (1 Corinthians 2:14).

2. *Knowledge.* "And find the knowledge of God." Purposeful study along the above lines will do more than merely give us the facts of the Bible; we will learn to know God. The divine personality will reveal himself. We know the living Word as we understand His revelation given to us in the written Word.

The study of the Bible is both like and unlike the study of other literature. It is like other studies in that it requires personal diligence and application. It is unlike the study of human literature in that it includes a spiritual as well as an intellectual element. The Holy Spirit is the Author of the Book, and He must be its Interpreter.

Language is the expression of thought. We know other people through communication. We get to know the mind of God through the Word of God. There are depths of meaning, however, in God's written communication which can only be seen by Spirit-anointed eyes. By this supernatural means we see the Word as more than mere literature, for the Holy Spirit "will guide you into all truth" (John 16:13).

Jesus himself will open our understanding. Luke 24 is the chapter of openings. There the Lord opened the Scripture to the two Emmaus disciples (vv. 27, 32). Their eyes were opened to know Him (v. 31). And then He "opened ... their understanding, that they might understand the Scriptures" (v. 45).

Understanding in the study of the Scriptures does not originate within us. Understanding comes from God. Enlightenment does not depend upon us; it comes through the Holy Spirit. The Psalmist declares, "For thou wilt light my candle: the Lord my God will enlighten my darkness" (Psalm 18:28). God is the One who reveals. "Thou hast hid these things from the wise and prudent, and hast revealed them unto babes" (Matthew 11:25). "Open thou mine eyes, that I may behold wondrous things out of thy law" (Psalm 119:18). "Make me to understand the way of thy precepts" (Psalm 119:27).

The Bible itself will give us understanding and light. It does not necessarily come all at once, but it will come as we study. "The entrance of thy words giveth light; it giveth understanding to the simple" (Psalm 119:130). Understanding comes as we allow the entrance of the Word into our hearts and minds. Never allow the Word entrance into your innermost being and you will never have understanding in it. "Through thy precepts I get understanding" (Psalm 119:104).

God has promised that "His secret is with the righteous" (Proverbs 3:32). "The secret of the Lord is with them that fear him; and he will show them his covenant" (Psalm 25:14). These verses make it very clear. Those who are righteous in Christ—those who fear or reverence God—will see and understand His covenant, which is His Word. While the sinner does not understand or know, the person who is born again can, for God gives the believer the spiritual awakening and capacity to know and understand.

The Christian who is willing to do God's will is assured of understanding the doctrine or teachings of Scripture. "If any man will do his will, he shall know of the doctrine" (John 7:17). The Bible will soon become dry and of little interest to those who habitually disregard the riches He graciously reveals to them through the study of His Word.

You Hold the Key

The believer himself holds the key to the effectiveness of the Bible in his life. Christian growth is open to every individual when he turns to Christ in Bible study.

The first key reduces itself to the willingness of the follower of Christ to know what the Bible teaches. He comes to this decision because he recognizes that God has commanded him to "desire the sincere milk of the word" (1 Peter 2:2) and to "study to show [himself] approved unto God, a workman that needeth not to be ashamed, rightly dividing the word of truth" (2 Timothy 2:15). He discovers that only the Word of God can give him that which he needs for daily strength, spiritual growth, and Christian living.

The next key is the willingness to give time to Bible study. One will never know the Bible unless he is willing to take the needed time to mine its riches. Priority must be given to regular, systematic study.

The third key is the willingness to keep at it. Despite interruptions, hindrances, and the tricks of Satan, the Christian who wants to unlock the treasures of God's Word will constantly keep at it.

Our Heavenly Father wants us to study His Word. He has given us the Book and the Teacher. There is an abundance of help in the way of Bible study books and study methods. But in the final analysis the believer himself holds the key. He must desire to know the Scriptures, be willing to take the needed time, and resolve to persevere in the face of every obstacle.

2

Interpreting the Bible

ALL BIBLE-BELIEVING CHRISTIANS agree that God has spoken in His Word. It follows naturally to ask what He has said. We do not profit if we do not know what He has said. This is the basic task of Bible interpretation, otherwise known as hermeneutics.

Ancient interpreters closed their eyes to the human elements of the Bible, all the while accepting it as a divine Book. They regarded the Bible as an archive of divine sayings. Mistakenly, they tried to confirm their speculations and theories by it. The tragic result was that the Scriptures were taken from the common people. Among the Jews none but a rabbi was considered capable of interpreting the Old Testament. Later in the Christian centuries many believed that only the church hierarchy could properly interpret the Scriptures. During the Reformation the Scriptures were freed from the bondage of church tradition.

WHEN CHRISTIANS DISAGREE

When two men, apparently led by the Holy Spirit, differ on the meaning of a Bible verse or passage, it leaves some people with a feeling of bewilderment. Most Christians can understand differences that arise between Bible believers and skeptics. By the science of apologetics the scoffers are met on their own terms. On the other hand, when it is not a question of unbelief but rather one of interpretation, we look to the science of hermeneutics, which simply means interpretation. The Greek word *diermeneuo*, translated "interpreted" in the New Testament, is essentially the same from which the word *hermeneutics* is derived. Hermeneutics is, then, the science of interpretation.

THE SCIENCE OF INTERPRETATION

Hermeneutics, or interpretation, is a true science and therefore has defined laws. To violate law is to invite error and failure. This is true whether the matter before us is solving a mathematical problem, a scientific theory, a Bible proposition, or even such a simple matter as baking a cake.

The interpretation of the Bible is an exciting science. Knowledge of the Hebrew and Greek languages, of history, of geography, and of other general areas of knowledge can prove helpful. But one does not need to be a scholar to learn to interpret the Bible correctly. The Bible is not a closed book, shrouded in mystery. God meant it to be read, studied, and understood. This can be a fascinating experience for anyone.

The Bible is a divine Book, but it is phrased in human language. The Bible is made up of words "which the Holy Ghost teacheth" (1 Corinthians 2:13), and these words are understood only in their relation to each other. This is only one of many principles of Bible interpretation. To find agreement on interpretation we must first agree on the principles of interpretation.

The foremost need of correct Bible interpretation is to determine how the Scriptures are to be understood that we may know what God has said. Without this the Bible can become a source of confusion. Because improper interpretation has been used, men have sanctioned the practice of polygamy since the Old Testament patriarchs did. Or, because the Old Testament sanctioned the death of witches, we may do the same.

The systems of interpretation employed by the camps of orthodoxy, neo-orthodoxy, and liberalism have very important differences. The only way to determine what is right and wrong, orthodox and heretical, is to understand the science of Bible interpretation. Otherwise we debate about the superstructure when we should debate about the foundations.

The next great need for sound Bible interpretation is to span the gap between our minds and the minds of the writers of Scripture. By no means would we imply that one has to be trained in language, culture, geography, and history to understand the Bible. But we must remember that figures of speech used by the people of Bible times are part of the Biblical narrative. This includes the metaphor, the simile, the parable, the symbol, the allegory, and the type. An understanding of these and similar cultural patterns of various Biblical periods greatly aids us in our understanding of the Bible. An understanding of the geography of Bible lands and historical backgrounds is very helpful. References to towns, places, rivers, mountains, seas, lakes, plains become more meaningful as we get them in geographical perspective.

A PENTECOSTAL-PROTESTANT PREMISE

Pentecostals subscribe to the basic Protestant principle that God chose to reveal himself in the Scriptures in a realistic way. Otherwise, what God has said would be hidden to all but a few. Therefore, the Bible student will take the language of the Scripture seriously, understood in terms of the historical situation in which the author wrote. This is known as the grammatico-historical approach to hermeneutics. This realistic approach must by no means take away the value of the devotional approach to the Bible by which a person may, in his meditation, find God speaking to him from isolated passages for inspiration and help for a given day or specific need. This latter, however, is not necessarily interpretation, but rather immediate personal encounter with God for that hour.

We tend to interpret Scripture according to our preconceived notions. It is very easy to become biased. We are inclined to interpret the Bible in the way most favorable to what we want to believe or the way best suited to the manner in which we want to live. How then can we know what is right interpretation?

The Bible is a book that requires reading, rereading, then another reading, and rereading over and over again. And the message is never exhausted. The depth of its truths goes beyond the penetrating power of the greatest mind. Yet there are the great truths of the plan of salvation which are plain and clear. The Christian is under obligation to read, to study, and to understand the Word of God.

PREREQUISITES FOR AN INTERPRETER

Spiritual things are spiritually discerned. The carnal mind is at enmity with God; the regenerate, spiritual mind alone can be at home with God and His Word (1 Corinthians 2:14). Pascal said, "Human knowledge must be understood to be loved, but divine knowledge must be loved to be understood."

The first prerequisite of the interpreter is the new birth experience. Angus and Green state, "This first principle of Bible interpretation is taken from the Bible itself. It occupies the same place, too, in the teaching of our Lord, who, in His first recorded discourse, assured Nicodemus that 'except a man be born again, he cannot see'—can neither understand the nature nor share the blessedness—of the kingdom of God." With the experience of the new birth comes a direct contact with the Holy Spirit, the revealer of God's truth. The eyes are opened to behold the Saviour. When the Holy Spirit enables us to see Jesus, the living Word, He also makes it possible for us to see Him and His truth in the written Word.

The second prerequisite is a devoted heart. We must possess an insatiable desire to know and understand the Bible. The Psalmist says, "But his delight is in the law of the Lord; and in his law doth he meditate day and night" (Psalm 1:2).

The third prerequisite is an abiding reverence for God and His Word. Humility of spirit and childlike trust are needed. Jesus said, "I thank thee, O Father . . . because thou hast hid these things from the wise and prudent, and hast revealed them unto babes" (Matthew 11:25). Reverence for God will be accompanied by obedience to His instructions. God does not reveal His truth to those who are unwilling to obey (John 7:17).

Finally, there must be absolute dependence upon the Holy Spirit. He is the key to the understanding of the Bible. The Holy Spirit inspired holy men of old to pen the Word. He is available today to reveal the truth of that Word to men who are yielded to Him.

The Christian has an additional dimension available to him. Any experience in the Holy Spirit is wonderful, but what can match the fullness of the Spirit? Paul prayed, "that ye might be filled with all the fulness of God" (Ephesians 3:19). When He fills and controls us, there will be an even more helpful and clear illumination of the Scriptures.

Note what Paul writes to the Corinthians: "For who among men knows a man's thoughts, except the man's own spirit within him? In the same way also only God's Spirit is acquainted with God's thoughts. But we have not received the spirit of the world, but the Spirit which comes from God, that we may know what is freely given us by God. This we also utter, not in language which man's wisdom teaches us, but in that which the Spirit teaches, adopting spiritual words to spiritual truths. The unspiritual man rejects the teachings of the Spirit of God: to him they are folly, and he cannot learn them, because they are spiritually appraised. But the spiritual man appraises everything, although he is himself appraised by no one" (1 Corinthians 2:11-15, Weymouth).

In summary, rules of hermeneutics are of little value without the above prerequisites. The interpreter must be born again, devoted, humble, obedient, teachable, and Spirit-led.

PRINCIPLES OF INTERPRETATION

The principles of Bible interpretation can be summarized under three headings for the purpose of simplicity. They are the ABCs of Bible interpretations—accuracy, background, and common sense. Keep these principles in focus, for they are essential as a guard against misinterpretation. Study the Bible with them in mind.

ACCURACY

To understand properly we must accurately identify all persons, places, events, and objects appearing in the passage. Further, all words should be accurately defined.

To illustrate, there are two Antiochs: one, the capital of Syria and a center of missionary activity, the place where disciples were first called Christians (Acts 11:19-26); the other, Antioch in Pisidia, a city in Asia Minor (Acts 13:14-52; 14:19-21). Chinnereth, Gennesaret, and Tiberias are other names for the Sea of Galilee.

There are six Marys mentioned in the New Testament: the Virgin Mary (Matthew 1:18); Mary, the wife of Cleophas (John 19:25; Mary Magdalene (Matthew 27:56); Mary of Bethany, sister of Martha and Lazarus (John 11:1); Mary, mother of Mark (Acts 12:12); and Mary, a Christian woman in Rome (Romans 16:6). There are three men named James, 10 different Simons, and four or five men named John. Peter was also called Simon and Cephas. Matthew also bore the name of Levi. Jacob was renamed Israel.

We must also be sure to consider the true meaning of words. Some words of the older Bible versions are obsolete or have completely changed in meaning. Let us illustrate from 2 Thessalonians 2:7: "For the mystery of iniquity doth already work: only he who now letteth will let, until he be taken out of the way." The word *let* meant "hinder" in 1611; now it means "permit, allow." Note another example: the word *conversation* as it appears in such passages as Philippians 1:27 and Hebrews 13:5 meant "manner of life," "behavior," in 1611, whereas today it means "speech." For this reason modern translations are helpful. Some study Bibles give the modern translations in center column references or in notes.

The speakers and the writers of Scripture illustrated their messages and writings with expressions of contemporary interest. Common articles of their day were used. An understanding of manners and customs of that day brings understanding to passages such as, "Neither do men put new wine into old bottles" (Matthew 9:17). One needs to study Bible history, Bible customs, and Bible geography to appreciate the significance and meaning in the illustrations.

BACKGROUND

A text without a context is a pretext, and therefore Scripture, whether a word, a verse, a passage, or even a book, must be seen in its proper relationship. We do not honor the Bible when we make it a collection of texts that may be lifted from the sacred page at our pleasure and used in any way we see fit, for isolated passages taken out of their context are often misleading. Each verse is set in its proper context or setting, and the context generally holds the key to the meaning of that passage.

"That you can prove anything by the Bible" is true only if words are lifted out of their proper setting. Psalm 14:1 states, "There is no God," if we take it out of its setting. But the whole verse reads, "The fool hath said in his heart, There is no God." Or was Paul recommending a meatless diet when he said, "I will eat no flesh while the world standeth"? (1 Corinthians 8:13). No, he was talking about abstaining from meat offered to idols and causing a brother to stumble.

From the Bible it can be shown that we should go and hang ourselves. We are told in Matthew 27:5 that Judas "went and hanged himself." In Luke 10:37 we read, "Then said Jesus . . . Go, and do thou likewise." Jesus said in John 13:27, "That thou doest, do quickly." All will agree that this is wresting Scripture completely out of its meaning to the extent of being ridiculous. But it illustrates the error of taking a collection of texts that we may lift at pleasure to use in any way we wish. This is never fair, whether the treatment is of a man's address or conversation or an author's book. The unfair practice of quoting people out of context is often a basis for misunderstanding and even character assassination. Think of how God's Word is dishonored by this practice.

We honor the Bible when we take it as it stands, and when we interpret each verse and each word in the light of the total message. To illustrate, the Bible contains the words of Satan in passages such as Job 1:9-11; 2:4, 5, and of the enemies of God and His people in passages such as Isaiah 36, where Rabshakeh counseled the people of Judah to surrender to Sennacherib, king of Assyria.

To the evangelist Luke, "the world" was the Roman world. When he speaks of a decree from Caesar Augustus that "all the world should be taxed" (or "enrolled") we are reminded of the vastness of the Roman Empire under Augustus, but we should not think of including India or China in that "world" in which the decree of Augustus was binding (cf. Luke 2:1).

Scriptural promises and commands must be interpreted in the light of their context. God's command for Jeremiah not to marry (Jeremiah 16:1-4) is not an argument for celibacy. It is interpreted by the context. The social life of Judah was about to become disrupted and to cease in the land. Later the exiles in Babylon were urged to marry and raise children (Jeremiah 29:4-7). The command becomes meaningful in the light of the total picture.

We must bear in mind that chapter divisions and even verse divisions are imperfect, for they are the work of man. They are very helpful for identification purposes, but to avoid confusion we must consider them in the light of their context.

The meaningful passage describing the humiliation, suffering, and glorification of Christ in Isaiah 53 really has its beginning in verse 13 of chapter 52. The first verse of Colossians 4 could well belong to the third chapter.

Each verse should be studied in the light of the entire chapter, or better yet, in the light of the unit of particular truth. Each chapter should be treated in the light of the entire book.

Keep the following items in mind as background for a particular passage:

1. *The speaker*. Who is speaking—God, an apostle, a prophet, a saint, a sinner, an angel, or Satan? What is the character of

the speaker? If he is a man, what is his age, his experience, his background? The "lad" Isaac who trudged with his father Abraham into the land of Moriah to be offered as a sacrifice was a full-grown man. Many do not realize that Daniel was about 90 years old, not a young man, when he was thrown into the den of lions.

2. *The addressee.* To whom are the words addressed—God, man, saint, sinner, backslider, individual, or a group?

3. *The time.* When was it spoken? To illustrate, several of the prophets of the Old Testament were contemporaries. Amos and Hosea prophesied to the Northern Kingdom at the time Isaiah and Micah brought God's message to Judah. While Daniel witnessed to royalty in Babylon, Ezekiel sat with the captives by the river Chebar, and Jeremiah ministered to the remnant left in the ruins of Jerusalem.

4. *The place.* Paul wrote to the Ephesians of "blessings in heavenly places" and to the Philippians he said, "For I have learned, in whatsoever state I am, therewith to be content." These passages become particularly meaningful when we bear in mind that both letters were written from prison.

5. *The main theme.* Bear in mind the occasion and the main subject of the passage. The principle will help us understand a passage such as "Work out your own salvation with fear and trembling" (Philippians 2:12). The passage does not teach that salvation and heaven are earned by works. The theme of the chapter is Christian living, and the letter itself was addressed to those who were Christians (1:1).

Do not interpret a verse or a passage as an isolated piece of Scripture. Study it in its proper setting with all the passages related to it. This will solve many of the seeming contradictions over which some people struggle.

COMMON SENSE

The ingredient of common sense is subjective. Its significance lies in the fact that, due to their attitude toward the Scriptures, many are overcome by a peculiar outlook which causes them to leave their common sense outside the door when they enter the sanctuary of Biblical interpretation. As a result, they look for trick or magical explanations. They are not content to accept the obvious meaning of the text; they must find something sensational in it. Imagery is taken literally, and literal statements are construed figuratively. No place is allowed for the use of hyperbole. If the newspaper were read in this manner, the outcome would be disastrous.

The only antidote for these dangerous practices is to remind oneself of the need for plain common sense in the interpretation of the Scriptures.

It should be stressed that the principle of common sense, like every good thing, is capable of misapplication. It may become the means of lowering divine standards to meet human standards. It may be used as an excuse for failing to heed scriptural exhortations. However, the presence of these dangers ought not to hide the validity of the principle itself and ought only to motivate one to be careful in its application.

The Bible usually means exactly what it says. The Bible is the Word of God written in the language of men, and that language was meant to be understood. Any attempt to find hidden, obscure meanings is a denial of its value and can lead to error. As a rule, the Bible means what it appears to mean. The Spirit who inspired it wanted it to be understood. Wherever possible interpret the Bible literally. Augustine, one of the Early Church leaders, said, "When the plain sense of Scripture makes common sense, seek no other sense." Therefore, we need to take every word at its primary, usual, ordinary, literal meaning unless the facts of the context, studied in the light of related passages and established truths, indicate clearly otherwise.

LITERAL . . . FIGURATIVE

A problem for interpreters is the confusion over what is literal and what is figurative. The Bible is filled with figures of speech, such as metaphors and similes. It is a piece of literature and should be used as such. We must recognize figures of speech when we see them. For example, we read, "Moab is my washpot; over Edom will I cast out my shoe" (Psalm 60:8). While this is God speaking, common sense tells us that this is figurative language, for it does not mean that God literally washes himself or that He wears shoes.

When one studies the Bible he should not try to make it a kind of wonder book, a spiritual museum. In 1611, when the King James Version was translated, Shakespeare was 46 years old. Some "wise" person turned to the 46th Psalm and found the 46th word from the beginning was "shake" and the 46th word from the end of the Psalm was "spear." This was supposed to mean something or other.

Veterans Day is observed annually. Originally it was known as Armistice Day. The armistice to World War I was signed on the 11th day of the 11th month. A "wise" person turned to the 11th book, the 11th chapter, the 11th verse of the Bible which is 1 Kings 11:11, "This kingdom was rent from Solomon." The "wise" person said, "Therefore, it must be rent from Wilhelm." Of course, the next verse says that it will be rent from Solomon's son. This was supposed to be a prophecy to that effect.

This, then, is the absurd way in which people will sometimes spiritualize the Scriptures and will not even recognize figures of speech.

FIGURES OF SPEECH

Every language has its particular idioms. Metaphors, similes, and other figures of speech, while perplexing to others, are familiar in one's own language. Common examples in English include "ice water in his veins," "neat as a pin," "slick as glass."

The Bible employs many figures of speech. Written by Eastern men, it uses methods of expression and alludes to customs common to those areas of the world. The history and teachings of the Bible are also from a culture of 20 centuries ago. An understanding of Oriental expressions will be most helpful to us.

The most commonly used figure of speech in the Bible is the metaphor. A metaphor is a figure of speech in which a word or a phrase literally denoting one kind of object or idea is used in place of another to suggest a likeness or analogy between them. For example, "a ship plows the sea," or "he used a volley of oaths." Note a few of these fascinating figures of speech: "Ye are the salt of the earth" (Matthew 5:13); "I am the light of the world" (John 8:12); "I am the door" (John 10:9); "I am the bread of life" (John 6:35); "The Lord is my shepherd" (Psalm 23:1); "The name of the Lord is a strong tower" (Proverbs 18:10).

Another figure of speech is the simile, which brings two objects into comparison to show their similarity. A few of these from daily usage will illustrate: "black as soot"; "white as snow"; "smooth as silk." Scriptural usages of the simile can be illustrated by Paul's portrayal of the Christian as a soldier in Ephesians 6:10-20. The Christian's activities and resources are presented in picturesque manner as the believer's life is compared to warfare. His armor, his foes, and his source of power are described.

The Bible employs hyperbole on numerous occasions, which is exaggeration for effect and is used legitimately as a symbolic term. One of several is found in Matthew 7:3, "And why beholdest thou the mote that is in thy brother's eye, but considerest not the beam that is in thine own eye?"

Another category of the figures of speech used in the Scripture includes types, parables, and allegories.

Types are found in the Old Testament with fulfillment in the New. A type can be described in the words of Scripture: "A shadow of things to come" (Hebrews 10:1; Colossians 2:17). The type and the antitype do not agree in all things. Instead of identity there is similitude.

The Bible portrays truth by the use of parables. A parable is a comparison, specifically a short fictitious narrative from which a moral or spiritual truth is drawn, such as the parables of Jesus.

An allegory is similar to a parable, only perhaps not capable of literal interpretation. A question arises—how to distinguish allegory from fact? The safest rule in understanding Scripture is to take it literally unless there is a clear indication, either from the context or by comparison with some other part of the Bible, that it is to be understood figuratively. Common sense tells us that when Jesus said, "I am the door," He did not mean He was a literal door.

Scripture must be compared with Scripture. The Bible presents all sides of truth, and all Scripture must be considered, for seldom does a single passage contain the entire teaching on a subject. Contradictions disappear as study continues. To illustrate, Paul states that salvation is by faith (Romans 4:5), while James says, "By works a man is justified, and not by faith only" (James 2:24). Both are right. Faith is by faith alone, and James warns against an alone faith. One condemns works without faith, the other faith without works.

We arrive at proper interpretation by studying parallels of passages, of words, and of general teachings.

Finally, Bible interpretation should never be considered a purely mechanical or intellectual process, for it must involve the Holy Spirit. Samuel Taylor Coleridge said, "The Bible without the Spirit is a sundial by moonlight." If we are to know the message of the Bible and to rightly divide it, we need the aid of the heavenly interpreter, the Holy Spirit, who has promised to lead us into all truth.

Erroneous Interpretation

In order to elucidate further what is involved in accurate exposition, an attempt will be made to enumerate and discuss briefly some of the fallacious interpretive approaches that have been employed in the history of the Christian Church. It should be noted that each of these contains some truth or is motivated by at least a partially legitimate cause.

FRAGMENTARY INTERPRETATION

The fragmentary interpreter treats the Scriptures as if they are merely a collection of isolated verses, each of which may be understood apart from its immediate and broad context. Such a practice is partly due to the rather arbitrary division of the Bible into chapters and verses. Furthermore, there arise occasions when it is not possible to quote long passages, and it is much simpler and convenient to utilize a verse or two. This sometimes leads to the neglect of the contextual setting of Biblical statements.

DOGMATIC INTERPRETATION

This kind of exposition seeks support in the Scriptures for certain dogmas which have already been accepted. As a result, the Bible is explained so as to substantiate certain beliefs, and other possible interpretations are arbitrarily rejected. Such an approach often relates to fragmentary exposition using proof texts torn from their contexts to support certain dogmas. Both the fragmentary and dogmatic approaches illustrate the fact that Scripture can be used to prove anything.

Both of these erroneous kinds of interpretation, however, have an element of truth in them, for they accept the principle that the Bible should be appealed to as the authority for what the Christian believes. But they fail to examine carefully the true meaning of the authority of Scripture. The Scriptures are really authoritative only if they are used as the basis for formulating one's beliefs and not if they are merely employed to support one's dogmatic positions. The first approach begins with the Scriptures and moves to the Scriptures. In the first case the Bible is the actual authority; in the second instance the individual is the actual authority. The former approach is objective and valid; the latter is subjective and invalid. In brief, the first is doctrinal, for it seeks in the Scriptures the beliefs it contains; the second is dogmatic, for it involves the assertion of tenets for which Biblical support is sought.

RATIONALISTIC INTERPRETATION

The rationalist attempts to expound the Bible in such a way as to make it acceptable to the reason. The inability to believe certain Biblical facts, such as miracles, often results in rationalistic interpretation. The rationalist needs to be made aware that man's reason is finite, and that the Scriptures can therefore never be emptied of their mystery.

MYTHOLOGICAL INTERPRETATION

The mythological approach is closely related to the preceding type in that it is often an expression of rationalism. Frequently, in order to remove that which cannot be comprehended or accepted by the reason, one will declare that certain events are myths rather than actual historical occurrences.

Such an approach serves to remove to a great extent the historical aspect of Scriptures by insisting that there is no indispensable relation between history and the conveyance of spiritual truth.

HISTORICAL INTERPRETATION

The opposite view from the one just described is the purely historical approach to the Scriptures. Some study the Bible as merely the history of certain peoples. This approach fails to realize that the Scriptures contain more than history; they involve history with spiritual implications and with a spiritual purpose. The history is the means to an end. One cannot therefore limit study to an examination of the means. One must also become aware of the objective to discover the full meaning of the Scriptures.

The historical view, however, reminds us that the Biblical message has a historical foundation.

ALLEGORICAL INTERPRETATION

The allegorical view is often used, for example, in the explanation of the parables. Instead of expounding them as parables, that is, as extended similes, those who use this approach interpret them as allegories or extended metaphors. Consequently, every detail is pressed for spiritual meaning.

However, a more dangerous form of allegorical explanation concerns the treatment of historical narratives. Those who utilize the allegorical approach frequently accept such narratives as historical; but, instead of expounding their meaning in view of their concrete historical settings, they use them as allegories to teach spiritual lessons. And, although the lessons drawn from them frequently are true because they are based on a general awareness of the Biblical message, they have no organic relation to the historical narratives being explained. Such an approach, to say the least, is very enticing but is also deceptive.

If this is true, then the basic question which should concern the interpreter is this: What means was the author utilizing and what was his purpose in recording these events? An author may use one of two ways to convey spiritual lessons. He may employ the historical approach, which is direct, or the parabolic or allegorical approach, which is indirect. The primary problem of the expositor is to discover which of these the writer was employing and to interpret accordingly. If he was utilizing the direct method, the expositor should utilize the direct method. If he was utilizing the indirect approach, then the expositor should also utilize the indirect approach.

TYPOLOGICAL INTERPRETATION

Those who practice this approach expound the Old Testament as if at every point it foreshadows the New Testament. Even the most minute details in historical narratives are often interpreted as types which are fulfilled in the New Testament.

Such a view begins with the legitimate principle that the Old Testament reveals the New, and that an important aspect of this revelation involved the use of certain symbolic practices to equip Israel to understand the coming and meaning of Christ. The sacrificial system of Leviticus affords an excellent example of these. However, it does not follow that every detail of the Old Testament is a type of the New.

CROSS REFERENCE INTERPRETATION

Some approach the Scriptures as a maze of cross references. They constantly search for similar passages. They explain each passage in the light of comparable ones. In so doing, they often fail to take time to examine each unit to discover its singular meaning, and therefore frequently make erroneous associations. The result is much faulty interpretation.

LITERARY INTERPRETATION

Many who purportedly examine the Scriptures from the standpoint of great literature fail to take into account the fact that purpose is essential to greatness in literature. They search the Bible merely for its euphonious phrases and picturesque images, as if it were a purposeless collection of appealing expressions and no more.

How much more valid it is to proceed on the basis that the Bible consists of great literature, not only because its literary form is worthy of praise, but also because it has a great purpose. This approach recognizes the fact that, though literary form is important, it is a means to an end, and that literature must be studied on the basis of both means and end.

3

Using Tools

THE MOST IMPORTANT BOOK to use in the study of the Bible is the Bible itself. Too many people read many books about the Bible but read the Bible itself very little. True Bible study must begin with the Book, for the Bible itself is primary.

All of us have searched for an elusive verse. We remember it as being in Matthew—or perhaps Mark, or Luke—or was it in John? We can quote it verbatim but we cannot locate it by chapter and verse.

Another problem is learning the meaning of a verse that is obscure by the customs and languages of Bible times. Really, is it easier "for a camel to go through the eye of a needle, than for a rich man to enter into the kingdom of God"? (Matthew 19:24)

Still another question: how tall was Goliath, "whose height was six cubits and a span"? (1 Samuel 17:4). How do you translate Bible measurements into present-day standards?

There are several basic reference books that can help in the problems that arise in our Bible study. For hundreds of years accurate, detailed work has been done in developing helps for using and understanding the Bible. Any serious, systematic study of the Bible will demand a certain minimum of study helps. This chapter presents a list of Bible study tools which scholars have produced to help you study.

What Translation Shall We Use?

A student of the Bible, and one who is a teacher of the Bible, may do well to build a Bible library. The question becomes—where shall I begin in securing the 'best translations?

The number of new English translations and paraphrases which have come on the scene in recent years has surpassed the total of many centuries. Gratefully we see renewed interest in Bible study. There have been over 500 translations of the English Bible in whole or in part since the King James translation in 1611, over 400 having been done in the past 100 years.

There is a difference between a translation and a paraphrase. Webster defines a translation as the "rendering from one language to another" of a given statement or text. A paraphrase is the restatement of a text already translated, giving the meaning in another form. It may include "translation with latitude." A paraphrase allows for more freedom of expression and is usually the work of one man.

As a rule each translation reflects to a certain degree the viewpoint of the translator. Translations produced by a group of scholars are more apt to achieve greater accuracy than those which are the work of one person. No doubt there are particular nuances of thought and nuggets of truth which can be drawn from almost any translation or paraphrase. Care must be exercised to discriminate and note where the theological bias of the translator may steer one off course.

One should possess at least two Bibles. One should have large print and wide margins suitable for study and the making of notes. Such Bibles can be secured which have a concordance, maps, a dictionary of proper names, and a subject index. The second Bible could be smaller and more suitable for carrying with one. It seems self-defeating to encourage people to read the Bible and then lead them to purchase Bibles with print so small that reading is laborious.

According to a recent survey made by an evangelical publisher, 84 percent of their readers use the King James, otherwise known as the Authorized Version. Yet the modern language Bibles are widely used for leisure reading and for clarity of text. Every student will want to use a King James Version. It is unsurpassed for beauty of expression in the English language and is still the most commonly used Bible among the people.

In addition, one could well have a copy of the American Standard Version, which is an American revision of the 1881-1885 English revision of the King James, and one deeply appreciated by Bible scholars.

REFERENCE BIBLES

THOMPSON'S CHAIN REFERENCE BIBLE

This thorough and helpful work has a host of notes in the margin and an excellent section of "Condensed Encyclopedia . . ." divided into over 7,000 topics. It also contains information on the canon and the principal English versions, an outlined analysis of each book, maps, a concordance, and an index. It also has a good harmony of the Gospels and excellent charts.

SCOFIELD REFERENCE BIBLE

This is a much used reference. The text is prominent in bold type, with comments at the foot and numerous synopses on various subjects. Some of the notes are excellent, others are not perfect, and some are unacceptable to many. In places the comments are strongly Calvinistic. Unlike a number of other Bibles, it is not self-pronouncing.

In 1967 a revised edition of this Bible was published. It retains the King James text, but archaic and obsolete words have been eliminated, causing the revision of some sentences. To illustrate, 2 Corinthians 6:11-13 now reads, "O ye Corinthians, our speech to you is candid, our heart is wide open. On our part there is no constraint, but there is constraint in your affections. In fair exchange . . . open wide your hearts to us." Margins are enlarged, cross-references increased, footnotes renumbered, book introductions enlarged and corrected where necessary, and the Ussher chronology has been eliminated. The dispensational system remains, but in a modified form.

DIXON ANALYTICAL EDITION

This Bible contains a dictionary, concordance, topical study, chronology, outlines and outstanding facts of each book, and information on the canon and various versions. References are footnoted below each verse, and revisions are bracketed in the verses.

Other reference Bibles could include the *New Oxford Reference Bible* and the *Holman Study Bible. The Englishman's Bible*, by Thomas Newberry, has blessed many. It has marks and signs meant to give the ordinary English reader the full sense of the original Hebrew and Greek. The maps and charts of the tabernacle and temple, with explanatory notes, are valuable. *The Emphasized Bible*, by Rotherham, particularly the Old Testament notes, is useful as a study book.

EARLIER MODERN TRANSLATIONS

Moffatt's translation has many brilliant insights, but the liberal theology of the author shows on occasion.

Weymouth's translation is clear, simple, dignified, and sound from a doctrinal viewpoint.

Goodspeed's translation tends to be liberal.

Williams' work is valuable, particularly in the translation of the Greek tenses.

Montgomery's work has been rated by some as one of the finer modern translations.

The Berkeley Version is quite conservative and more literal than Phillips', though modern. It contains a full set of footnotes.

Way's work borders on being interpretive.

NEWER MODERN TRANSLATIONS

The New American Standard Bible (NASB) is regarded by many scholars as the most accurate English translation available since 1963.

The New English Bible (NEB) is a fresh translation, not a revision. It was hailed when published in 1961 as the successor to the King James Version by some, while others disapprove of it on the ground that some important passages combine translation with objectionable interpretation. The translators claim it to be a free translation, but it is apparently admitted that it has at least in part the character of a paraphrase and of a commentary or interpretation.

Good News for Modern Man presents the New Testament in "Today's English Version" (TEV). It uses words and forms of English of contemporary style, giving it wide appeal to this generation. Debate continues over some of the specific words used, such as substituting "girl" for "virgin" in Luke 1:27 (in Matthew 1:23 TEV translates the same Greek word as "virgin"). It is also faulted for, in some instances, translating "death" instead of "blood," such as in Colossians 1:20; Hebrews 10:19; 1 Peter 1:19; and Revelation 1:5.

The New International Version of the New Testament (NIV) is hailed by conservative evangelicals as "clear, readable, yet accurate and true to the Greek . . . does not make unnecessary changes or extensive paraphrases. To a person brought up on the King James Version . . . it still sounds like the Bible."

EXPANDED TRANSLATIONS

Wuest's Expanded Translation is an interpretive translation as is the *Amplified*. Both are considered sound and helpful for study purposes.

PARAPHRASES

The Living Bible is, no doubt, the most popular paraphrase. Since it employs the use of current language of the layman rather than using a literal rendering of the original text, even to the extent of using colloquialisms, it appeals to the average reader. Phillips' Translation, a paraphrase, is picturesque. Its low-keyed prose is almost casual. For example, the familiar King James "holy kiss" (as in 1 Corinthians 16:20) becomes "shake hands all around." It communicates in a way that appeals to the modern reader instead of giving a literal translation.

PARALLEL TRANSLATIONS

Of interest to Bible students are volumes such as: *The New*

Testament from 26 Translations, The New Testament in Four Versions, and *The Six Version Parallel New Testament.*

Versions are necessary, particularly in view of language changes. Evaluation of versions involves consideration of their accuracy and usefulness. Accuracy is largely a matter for experts; usefulness is more a personal matter for the individual reader.

Great benefit comes from modern language translations. Read and enjoy them. Reading various modern translations will help to throw light on many Bible passages. But a word of caution should be observed. The majority of us cannot evaluate translations. Some translators have allowed their theological bias to enter into their translating work.

Marginal References

Although references in a Bible appear in various forms, the most common is the center reference column. Other methods are the side column reference, and references under each verse or at the bottom of the page.

The subject references lead the reader from the first clear mention of a truth to the last. In the *Scofield Reference Bible* the first and last references on the subject are in parentheses and are repeated each time. The reader can follow the subject from beginning to end at whatever point he finds it.

As an example, the word *gospel* appears in Romans 1:16. Next to the word is a small *a*. The *a* in the center column gives the word and its other appearances in the chapter (vv. 1, 9, 15). The next mention is in Romans 2:16, the first was in Genesis 12:1-3, and the last is in Revelation 14:6. The reference in Genesis 12:3 (small *e*) indicates the next reference in the chain is Isaiah 41:27. Thus an entire series of scriptural references on a given subject is tied together to give the reader what the Bible says on it.

Referring again to Romans 1:16 in the Scofield Bible, we find another study aid in the marginal reference column. By the word *salvation* is the numeral "1." The numeral leads one to the bottom of the page for a summary statement on the doctrine of salvation. This is typical of the footnotes to be found in this Bible.

Still another aid found in the reference column is an alternative rendering of a word or phrase. Let us illustrate from Acts 15:13-17. Verse 14 in the King James reads, "Simeon hath declared how God at the first did visit the Gentiles, to take out of them a people for his name." Turning again to the Scofield Bible, we find a literal rendering in the margin as follows: "God for the first time, i.e., in the house of Cornelius." The passage now becomes even more meaningful to Christians from among the Gentiles.

The margin also contains explanations of money, time, weights, etc. in many Bibles. General statistical, geographical, and language information also is given in some editions.

No particular edition is recommended. It is recommended, however, that one learn to use the marginal references, for they can be of great assistance.

CONCORDANCE

For many Christians the concordance is unfortunately only consulted to settle arguments in Bible games. But, next to the Bible itself, this is your most valuable tool for Bible study, for it provides immediate access to any verse of Scripture, if you remember only a part of it, even if but a word. Efforts are just beginning to develop concordances for other than the King James translation.

Three concordances are recognized leaders in the field: *Cruden's Unabridged Concordance; Young's Analytical Concordance to the Bible* (311,000 separate references to words and phrases in the Bible); and *Strong's Exhaustive Concordance of the Bible.* The latter two are more exhaustive. Personal references vary.

The *Englishman's Greek Concordance to the New Testament and the Hebrew and Chaldean Concordance to the Old Testament,* by Bagster, along with a Greek lexicon and Hebrew lexicon are valuable for advanced studies.

EXAMPLE OF CONCORDANCE USE

A concordance helps greatly to develop an understanding of a line of truth in the Bible. Note the following development on the topic of "Envy" as taken from *Young's Concordance* which lists 40 references (closely related words such as *covet* and *jealous* are not included).

1. SOURCES OF ENVY

A. When others are richer than we

Ecclesiastes 4:4—success of competitor
Genesis 26:14—Philistines envied Isaac's posessions
Genesis 30:1—barren Rachel envied fruitful Leah

B. When others are stronger than we

Genesis 37:4—Joseph envied by his brothers
Numbers 11:29—Joshua envied the two prophets

C. When others differ with us

1 Timothy 6:4—comes by strife
1 Corinthians 3:3—a sign of carnality

2. RESULTS OF ENVY

A. Separates friends and families

Isaiah 11:13
Ezekiel 35:11
Acts 7:9—caused brothers to sell Joseph
Philippians 1:15—divides preaching

B. Brings persecution and death

Acts 13:45; 17:5—against Paul
Matthew 27:18—brought death to Jesus

C. Is a deadly disease

Job 5:2—slays the foolish
Proverbs 14:30—rottenness of the bones
Proverbs 27:4—none can stand against it

3. CURE FOR ENVY

A. Put it from us

Psalms 37:1; 73:3, 16, 17; Proverbs 3:31; 24:1; Galatians 5:26; 1 Peter 2:1

B. Replace with the fear of the Lord

Proverbs 23:17

C. Replace with God's love by the Holy Spirit

1 Corinthians 13:4; Galatians 5:25, 26

BIBLE DICTIONARY AND ENCYCLOPEDIA

Have you wanted to study a custom of Bible days? Or to identify any place, person, or thing you read but don't understand? The answers for these and hundreds of other questions are to be found in a Bible dictionary. Like any dictionary it is an alphabetically arranged compilation of words and their definition, but they are words with Biblical significance. Included with proper nouns—the names of persons and places—are common nouns with scriptural meanings.

Through use of the dictionary and encyclopedia the student gets a clearer understanding of difficult words and unfamiliar names of persons, places, and things. The cubit is found to be a measurement of nearly 18 inches. The word *penny* is discovered to be the translation of the Greek word *denárion*, which was the chief Roman silver coin and was worth about 15 to 17 cents or the equivalent of a day's wages. The common noun *stone* is treated with its particular Biblical significance, with reference made to the places where the word appears. It will be found that the "hind" is a deer. The word *publican* is defined as the collector of Roman revenue, with detailed information regarding this class, hated among the Jews for their fraudulent exactions under the vicious system.

The use of a Bible dictionary and encyclopedia will bring a flood of light to the student. Among the better known works are *Davis' Dictionary of the Bible, Unger's Bible Dictionary, The New Bible Dictionary* by Douglas, *Smith's Bible Dictionary,* and the new *Pictorial Bible Dictionary* by Tenney. For a more exhaustive treatment of subject matter there is *The International Standard Bible Encyclopedia,* in five volumes, and the *Dictionary of the Bible* by Smith, in four volumes.

BIBLE ATLAS—BIBLE HISTORY

Where did Elijah go after slaying the prophets of Baal (1 Kings 18, 19)? Where was the Samaria Jesus had to go through? How far was it from Jerusalem to Babylon? Answers are found in a Bible atlas.

Though of secondary importance to the basic aids already listed, a Bible atlas or geography, a book on Biblical history, and a book on Bible manners and customs can make substantial contributions to Bible study.

A Bible atlas helps the student visualize the setting of great events of Scripture. As a source book of general information on Bible geography, geology, and archaeology, an atlas contains colored and outline maps and photographs.

The missionary journeys of Paul as recorded in Acts and the founding of churches by the apostle, along with his later epistles to the churches, take on enriched meaning to one who has knowledge of the geography of the lands involved. The same could be said for the journeys of Jesus, of Abraham, and others.

A good atlas is *Baker's Bible Atlas*. Others used by many include the *Oxford Bible Atlas*, the *Bible Atlas*, by Hurlbut, *The Land of Israel*, by Stewart, or the *Rand-McNally Bible Atlas*. (Conservatives, however, feel that the *Rand-McNally Bible Atlas* accepts liberal theories.) A larger work highly recommended is *The Historical Geography of the Holy Land*, by Smith. The same author has an accompanying *Historical Atlas of the Holy Land*.

A book on Biblical history such as *The History of Palestine and Syria to the Mohammedan Conquest*, by Olmstead, or *A Manual of Bible History, In Connection with the General History of the World*, by Blaikie, or *Lectures on the History of the Jewish Church*, by Stanley, are enlightening to bring history into focus.

Bible manners and customs shed light on the understanding of the Bible as revealed in books such as *The Land and the Book*, by Thompson.

A Bible handbook is a valuable tool to study. It may duplicate information in other types of books and could be a substitute to those who do not wish to invest in a number of books. *Halley's Bible Handbook*, as an example, is a mine of general Bible information, as are *Unger's Bible Handbook*, *Handbook to the Bible*, and the *Angus-Green Bible Handbook*.

Topical Textbook

One can use to good advantage for resource study books which arrange subjects in topical fashion. An example is *Torrey's Topical Textbook*, which lists 20,000 topics and subtopics and 30,000 Bible references.

Nave's Topical Bible is a sort of concordance with texts in full, a digest of 20,000 topics and subtopics, with 100,000 references to the Scriptures. Of this book Billy Graham states, "Outside of the Bible this is the book I depend on more than any other.... There is no book that has helped me more in my study ... I recommend it publicly in all campaigns and use it daily in my study and nightly from the platform."

Commentary

A Bible commentary, as implied by its name, comments on the Bible, passage by passage, and verse by verse, interpreting its meaning. For hundreds of years Bible scholars have recorded the results of their studies, and much of this has been gathered in commentaries. Some commentaries are the work of a single author, while others are a compilation of the efforts of a number of men. Commentaries may range in size from one to well over 50 volumes to a set.

Since a commentary is written to interpret Scripture, care should be taken in selecting a set. Three of the better known concise commentaries are *Matthew Henry's Commentary on the Whole Bible, Commentary on the Whole Bible* by Jamieson, Fausset and Brown, and *The Wycliffe Bible Commentary*.

A number of Bible study tools have been listed. Specific titles have been mentioned. The list is very limited and does not necessarily give the best title in a given field; it is only an attempt to help those who are interested in developing a Bible study library.

Bibles with explanatory notes are convenient and helpful, but no Christian should allow himself to read the notes and think he has studied the Bible. We cannot overemphasize the necessity of studying the Bible itself, independently of all notes and commentary.

Today's Christians have available more helpful books for Bible study than Christians of any previous decade. Believers need to use these valuable aids—Bible dictionaries, atlases, annotated Bibles, commentaries—with increased effort and enthusiasm in mining the rich treasures of the Word of God.

Possessing a shelf of good books for Bible study is commendatory. But this is not synonymous with Bible knowledge. The contents must be absorbed. The harvest of the labors of the best evangelical scholars will enrich our knowledge of God and His Word.

HINTS FOR TEACHING

Have members of the class bring various translations for comparative purposes. Use a concordance to trace some word, a Bible dictionary to define an obscure term, and the margin reference to locate related words.

4

Introducing Methods

THE HIDDEN DEPTHS OF SCRIPTURE will not be opened to the casual reader. Many people believe the Bible is a Book one can open at random and it will reveal its lode of rich treasures. Such a practice will reveal some truth to the superficial reader, but it will not give him the full message.

To understand the Word of God properly one must grasp a comprehensive picture of its fundamental purpose. The Bible requires study. Jesus urged us to "search the Scriptures." The word *search* is a strong word indicating the use of energy, diligence, and application to the task. The hunter searches for prey; the prospector searches for treasure; the geologist searches for oil; the police search for the lawbreaker; the posse searches for the lost child. In each instance effort is required, and it is directed toward a definite goal. In a similar manner we must employ thorough-going effort in searching the Scriptures.

Individual differences make it impractical for one person to force upon others a rigid formula for Bible study. Certain basic principles are essential if our approach is to be sound. Method must never be an end in itself; it merely forms a channel for the use of God-given mental abilities. Ultimate learning must come through the illumination of the Holy Spirit. The purpose of the mechanics used—and of this book—is that the user may through application of the principles outlined come to know the real Author of the Scriptures, the one true God, and His Son Jesus Christ in a better way.

There is no single, final approach to be executed conclusively at one sitting and which need never be repeated. No matter how valid a study process may be, it cannot be expected to consume the truth of a Scripture passage in one application. The Bible can be likened to an artesian well whose supply is inexhaustible, regardless of how much we drink of it. Further, our personal growth enables us to find more spiritual food in the Word today than yesterday and more tomorrow than today. And it is not necessary to understand everything. We are studying the Bible, not just to learn about it, but to live by it. What is necessary is to respond to what we do understand. Live by the light God gives us; and, as we continue to study and obey, the blessed Holy Spirit will shed more light on our path from day to day.

DEVOTIONAL STUDY

The close, analytical study of the Bible is an absorbing and a proper pursuit. But it must never be separated from a disciplined devotional life. The Bible must nourish the soul. In devotional study we are not searching for homiletical study, nor for research or analysis. That may develop, but it does not have priority. We come for spiritual food. Our souls are fed as the Word speaks to us. In meditation we find God's will and learn to know Him. There we learn to claim the promises. Scholarly study, paying attention to details, is essential, but we must always see the Bible for what it is—the actual Word of God which is "living, and powerful, and sharper than any two-edged sword . . . and is a discerner of the thoughts and intents of the heart" (Hebrews 4:12).

A young lady explained what was meant by devotional reading of the Bible by saying that she had just received a letter from one to whom she had given her heart. She had read the letter five times, not because she did not understand it at the first reading, not because of duty, not because of a desire to commend herself to the author. She read it over and over again because she was devoted to the one who wrote it. This illustrates the manner in which the Bible is studied devotionally. It will help us to maintain a spiritual glow and a loving devotion to our Lord.

The Word incarnate is revealed to us in the Word written, and the more we know of this written Word, the richer will be our knowledge of Christ, the living Word. The more we know Him, the more we love Him and the more we will obey Him. Is this not what He says in John's Gospel (15:7-11): "If ye abide in me, and my words abide in you, ye shall ask what ye will, and it shall be done unto you. Herein is my Father glorified, that ye bear much fruit; so shall ye be my disciples. As the Father hath loved me, so have I loved you: continue ye in my love. If ye keep my commandments, ye shall abide in my love; even as I have kept my Father's commandments, and abide in his love. These things have I spoken unto you, that my joy might remain in you, and that your joy might be full."

Regular Bible reading and study of a daily portion, whether a set amount, or time, or until you come to a verse on which you wish to meditate, will set the spiritual tone for the activities of your day.

The devotional method emphasizes the gaining of truth for personal spiritual need. All of God's truth was written not to prepare us for passing examinations as in school but for the purpose of living a life. Aside from all other considerations, in devotional study we ask ourselves, what does this passage, this verse say to my heart? Does it speak to a present need? How does it further reveal Jesus to me?

Three simple steps may be helpful. First, make the message plain. Second, make the message personal. Third, make the message practical. We find our answers in meditation. David writes about meditating in God's Word "day and night" (Psalm 1:1, 2) and prays that his "words ... and meditation" will be acceptable in God's sight (Psalm 19:14). Psalm 119 indicates the Psalmist's determination to meditate in God's Word (vv. 15, 23, 48, 78, 97, 99, 108). God commanded Joshua to "meditate ... day and night" in the Book of the Law (Joshua 1:8). Meditation comes from a Greek word meaning "to attend." In other words, we are to read with attention. Even more so, it is reading with intention.

It is important to notice that meditation is nowhere associated with ourselves or our sin. The Psalmist puts it in perspective, "my meditation of him" (Psalm 104:34). To be occupied with self is dangerous, with our sin is depressing, but with Him is glorious. Note it is my meditation, not another's; it is "of my heart" (Psalm 49:3).

The Psalmist prayed, "Open thou mine eyes, that I may behold wondrous things out of thy law" (119:18). In the light of this prayer let us look at the above-mentioned three steps.

Make the message plain. Jesus said, "Search the Scriptures" (John 5:39). We need to look. Look for things about God and His Son, their character, actions, purposes. Look for things about yourself. Look for commands, prayers, promises, warnings. Mark your Bible. Write in the margin. Use a notebook. For me, truth jotted down blesses me, not only for the moment, but grows on me in the days ahead.

Make the message personal. The Psalmist was personal (119: 105). Make your findings personal. Make the application to yourself. Put it in the first person singular. "I ought to be . . . do . . . God promises me . . . If I don't do . . . the consequence for me is . . ."

Make the message practical. The practical James illustrates this in his epistle (1:22-25). The message observed must be acted upon. If you have found something of personal application, make a decision. Chart a course of action. To agree to "I ought to forgive others" is useless unless I forgive John Doe for that act I have been holding against him. Devotional reading entails more than sentimental introspection. It is never made to appear like daydreaming. It is purposeful. Jesus ruled out forever introspection with our own inner self as unhealthy stimulation of our own emotions when He said, "Blessed are they that hear the word of God, and keep it" (Luke 11:28).

DEDUCTIVE BIBLE STUDY

"There are two main approaches open to the Bible student," writes Robert A. Traina. "One is deduction, which begins with generalizations and moves for their support to the particulars. By its very nature deduction tends to be subjective and prejudicial. It produces those who dictate to the Scriptures rather than those who listen to the Scriptures. In view of the objective character of scriptural literature, such an approach is not suited to the Bible and is therefore unmethodical."[1]

In deduction, the topic is supported by searching for all the appropriate, but possibly disconnected, passages in the Bible. This is the basis in a sense for topical teaching. The deductive approach is not disparaged, but it does make for the possibility of subjectivity and prejudgment. Deduction is the basis for "proof text" theology. In deductive Bible study one begins with his doctrinal beliefs and moves to the data (the Bible itself). Those who have been taught doctrine or tradition from childhood too often go to the Bible to support the opinions they already hold.

[1] *Methodical Bible Study* (New York: Ganis and Harris, 1952).

5

Getting the Overview

ONE OF THE BETTER METHODS of Bible study is Bible synthesis. This approach to understanding the Bible was made famous by the late Dr. James M. Gray, a former president of Moody Bible Institute.

Synthetic study simply means the study of the Bible as a whole, and each book of the Bible as a whole, and as seen in its relationship to the other books. Synthesis is the opposite of analysis. By analysis we take an object apart to examine its parts; by synthesis we "put it together and consider it as a whole."

In synthetic study you read a book to gain a comprehensive view of the whole. It can be likened to an explorer mounting the highest elevation to secure a general view of the surrounding country. Once the total message of a book has impressed itself upon you, the more detailed studies to follow will grow out of the framework you have established.

Synthetic study gives a comprehensive survey of the whole field. You get a broad sweep of the horizon and begin to feel the purpose and message of the Book.

Five simple rules were set forth by Dr. Gray for students interested in Bible synthesis:

1. Read the Bible, not books about the Bible. Such books are valuable in their proper place, but they cannot substitute for the Word itself. Reading is not study. The intial purpose is not to understand every paragraph or verse immediately in this approach even in

a second reading. Simply read naturally, but thoughtfully and prayerfully.

2. Read the book at a single sitting with disregard for chapter and verse divisions. In Bible synthesis you should not disrupt this reading to take it up again, for if you do you will lose the thread of truth which runs through the Book.

3. Read it repeatedly until you have the conscious possession of its outline. Truths which seem enshrouded in fog and appear to come out of the mist ever so little at first will become clear on the second or the sixth or the twelfth time. As opposed to devotional and inductive approaches in study, for purposes of Bible synthesis it is better to read rapidly rather than slowly.

4. Read it independently without the aid of tools such as commentaries.

5. Read it prayerfully dependent upon the Holy Spirit to give you understanding. When you pray as you read you are talking to the Author. The privilege of consulting the Author when engaged in the study of the Bible is a distinctive not available when studying other books.

Reading snatches of Scripture gives us no idea of the Bible, or any book in the Bible, as a whole, nor do we comprehend the great truths and doctrinal teachings of the Scriptures. The soul is fed, but the mind is not. Feeding the soul may be more important than feeding the mind, but both are necessary.

Content Before Interpretation

We must know the contents of Scripture before we can know its interpretation. In other words, we must know what the Bible says before we can know what it means. A first step will be to acquire a factual knowledge of the content of the Scriptures. Next we will need to see the unity of the Bible, the relationship of one book to another and of each to the whole. Then we will need to see Christ and His redemption in all the Bible. Finally, we must make personal application of the truths we have learned.

It is clear that, for our understanding, any text of the Bible must be seen in its context and against the background of the whole document. The thorough student will take as his task not the reading of a ready-made selection, but a complete document at a time. This will give him the dimension of perspective that cannot be received through selective readings. It will also give him balance. Heresy does not develop for the most part from the introduction of doctrinal untruth but from an emphasis of one aspect of doctrine at the expense of others.

After reading and rereading a book, at the same time jotting down your notes, you will sense its theme and purpose. You will want to establish who wrote it, to whom it was written, what was the occasion of the writing, and whether it relates in specific ways to other books. Without having some of these details in focus we may encounter difficulties in understanding.

AN OBJECT AND A SUBJECT

Every book in the Bible has an object as well as a subject. As a rule there is some key word, or verse, or phrase which gives us the clew and indicates the scope and purpose of the book.

The exceedingly expressive introduction of the Gospel of John loses some of its meaning unless we understand its purpose. The miracles performed by Christ as recorded by John are wonderful and faith inspiring, but they bring a new dimension as we understand why they were written. In like manner, the claims of our Lord speak more meaningfully when we realize that John lifts from the earthly life and ministry of Christ seven claims and seven supporting miracles for a specific purpose. "But these are written, that ye might believe that Jesus is the Christ, the Son of God; and that believing ye might have life through his name" (John 20:31).

Each book was written with a specific purpose in mind, and is intended to set forth doctrine and guard against error. Romans has as its great theme justification by faith, and the key phrase is "the righteousness of God." It was written in order to guard the Church against the error of salvation by works and lays a foundation for the Church and its doctrines. A grasp of Romans with its development of the great doctrine of justification by faith—the foundation truth of all Christian dogma—makes it possible for the believer to have a life of daily victory. Galatians was written to guard against ritualism and legalism. The Pentateuch lays a foundation of historical fact for the books that follow. And this pattern of specific purpose is true with other books.

SURVEY BEFORE ANALYSIS

Survey comes before analysis. First we look at the whole (the book in its entirety), then the parts (the chapter or logical divisions). Look at it in this manner, as pointed out by Irving L. Jensen:

FIRST	THEN
Image the whole	Execute the parts
Survey study	Analytical study
Skyscraper view	Ground level tour
Panoramic sweep	Microscopic focus

Jensen further states:

Knowing one's bearing in the forest of many facts is a tremendous help in Bible study. This is illustrated by an experience of Charles Lindbergh. On one of his early flights he lost a valuable instrument overboard. He watched it fall and land in the dense fields below. Later he landed a smaller plane in the general vicinity, and scoured the area by foot in search of the instrument, but to no avail. He resorted to a simple experiment. Taking off his coat, he spread it on a bush and returned to the air. From the air he saw both the coat and the instrument, and he made some mental notes of relationship and bearing. Landing again, he walked to the coat but still could not find the instrument. So he moved the coat to another bush and repeated the sighting from the air. With this additional bearing he was able finally to locate the instrument.[1]

When you read the Bible for purposes of study it is not enough to read one book and pass on to another. The same book must be read repeatedly—possibly a half-dozen or a dozen times—until the message grips you and begins to reveal its secrets to you. Many people read the Bible, even study it, but do not get a grip on it. They fail to gain a working

[1] *Enjoy Your Bible* (Chicago: Moody Press, 1969).

knowledge of its contents. To bypass this frustration, one can adopt a plan of reading, rereading, and reading again a book of the Bible until its message becomes a part of him. This will eventuate in his getting a grip on the book, or rather the book will get a grip on him.

Each of the New Testament epistles, except Romans, 1 and 2 Corinthians, and Hebrews, can be read in less than 30 minutes. If a person keeps this in mind, he will not be as easily discouraged at the task. Give Bible reading a fair chance and it will become fascinating as the Holy Spirit illuminates the Word. In devotional reading or inductive study we may pause for in-depth study of a verse, a phrase, or a word, but in Bible synthesis we read for the purpose of obtaining a sweeping view of the whole to grasp certain key information in the book.

When reading there are certain things to look for. It has been effectively expressed as follows:

> The author, scope, occasion, theme, time, place, and next
> The form: these seven let him attend that reads the text.

Your first readings may not leave much impression. But faithful, prayerful, systematic reading will not be fruitless. Soon details will begin to take shape in your mind. Persistent reading will give you familiarity with it and help you to use it freely.

Have you ever sat down and read the Gospel of Mark, for instance, right through at one sitting? It does not take long, and you will find a picture of the Lord and His gospel unveiled before you as the Holy Spirit intended Mark to portray. Certain expressions will become noticeable. Mark uses the terms *straightway* and *immediately*. These are keys to understanding. Mark pictures Jesus as the Servant, and the two characteristic expressions *straightway* and *immediately* are words of a servant. In similar manner, the word *better* is the key word in the Book of Hebrews, and is used to portray the contrast of the good things of Judaism and the better things of Christ. Other expressions include the term *precious* in the Petrine epistles and *they shall know that I am the Lord* in Ezekiel.

A knowledge of the author will prove helpful. To illustrate, a study of Paul, Peter, and John will reveal interesting facts about them. They could be called apostles of the three cardinal graces—faith, hope, and love. Paul might be called the apostle of faith, Peter the apostle of hope, and John the apostle of love. Note how their lives, their actions, and their writings emphasize these lines of truth.

To begin synthetic study, your book selection is important. A good starting point is Genesis, the book of beginnings. A beginner might well choose one of the shorter and simpler books of the New Testament, such as 1 John, or 1 Peter.

It is important that your study shall not be confined to "favorite" books. All of God's Word has something for us. Even if some book is laid aside for a time, do not neglect it altogether. There is no book that you can afford to leave out. If you do, you will fail to receive something God intended that you should know and have.

The synthetic method of study will help us to discover the scope of the book, to make a telescopic survey of its subject, to get a bird's-eye view of its whole with a resulting comprehensive idea of its plan, structure, content, and purpose. When difficult passages are seen in their proper place in the entire structure, their true meaning will be clear.

EXAMPLES OF SYNTHETIC STUDY

After repeated readings of any book of the Bible, one begins to see the aim of the author, and the contents begin to form an orderly pattern in his mind. Let us take a look at some examples.

THE BOOK OF GENESIS

Genesis is the book of beginnings. It records the beginning of the heavens and the earth, of plant, animal, and human life, and of human relationships and institutions.

Genesis records the history of Creation, the Fall, the Flood, and the beginning of nations. It relates the biography of Abraham, Isaac, Jacob, and Joseph.

The purpose of Genesis is to reveal God's will and purpose in creation and redemption from the time of Creation to the time of the beginning of His chosen nation, Israel.

The key word of Genesis is *generations,* which means "descendants, issue, posterity, that is, persons and things created or produced." The word occurs in the following instances: "generations of the heavens and of the earth" (2:4); "generations of Adam" (5:1); "generations of Noah" (6:9); "generations of the sons of Noah" (10:1); "generations of Shem" (11:10); "generations of Terah" (11:27); "generations of Ishmael, Abraham's son" (25:12); "generations of Isaac" (25:19); "generations of Esau" (36:1); "generations of Jacob" (37:2).

Certain facts stand in bold relief as we read Genesis. They bring a sweeping picture of the book.

The first great fact is Creation. This is covered in the first two chapters. Genesis 1 outlines the events of the six days of Creation: (1) light; (2) firmament; (3) dry land, sea, plant life; (4) sun, moon, and stars; (5) fish and fowl; (6) animals and man. The second chapter describes in greater detail the creation of man. This return to describe a matter in more detail is a pattern which the Holy Spirit uses again and again in the Bible. It is generally referred to as "the law of recurrence."

The second outstanding fact of Genesis is the Fall, the beginning of sin among men. Chapters 3 and 4 deal with this matter. Again one finds details that form an outline: the temptation of the serpent (3:1-5), the fall of Eve and Adam (3:6, 7), the seeking God (3:8-13), the curse (3:14-20), the provision of covering (3:21), the expulsion from Eden (3:22-24). Chapter 4 records the first murder and the first civilization.

The third great fact is the Flood, which is dealt with in chapters 5 through 9. Lesser details include the genealogy of Noah (chapter 5), the building of the ark (chapter 6), the Flood (chapter 7), the return to the land (chapter 8), and the covenant with Noah (chapter 9).

The fourth great fact is the beginning of nations (chapters

10 and 11). This was occasioned by the confusion of tongues as a result of God's judgment at Babel.

The fifth great fact is the call of Abraham. The Holy Spirit uses chapters 12 to 25 to record events relating to the life of Abraham. Again there is the list of lesser details, from the time of his call (12:1-3) to his death (25:7-10). Man had turned away from God. The Lord chose Abraham to father a chosen nation, Israel. From him came the lineage that provided the promised Redeemer. Of special note are the types of Christ and His redemption in these chapters—Melchizedek (14:18-20; compare Hebrews 7, Psalm 110) and the substitute ram offered in Isaac's stead (22:13, 14). The apostle Paul used Abraham as an illustration of justifying faith in Romans 4.

The biography of Isaac is the sixth great fact (chapters 21-28). Isaac is noteworthy as a type of Christ—a type in his birth which was both supernatural and predicted, a type in his sacrifice when offered by his father as an only son. His return from the place of sacrifice was a type of Christ's resurrection. The incidents surrounding his marriage to Rebekah offer several beautiful pictures of Christ and His bride.

The seventh major fact of Genesis is the history of Jacob (chapters 25-36). Major lessons to be learned from the life of Jacob are: (1) the grace of God as manifested on behalf of Jacob; (2) the illustration of prevailing prayer at Peniel; (3) God's estimate of faith, for Jacob received the Lord's blessing because of his appreciation of spiritual things; (4) when Laban cheated Jacob it bore out the fact that "Whatsoever a man soweth, that shall he also reap "

The last great fact is the biography of Joseph, to whom God saw fit to devote the greater part of 14 chapters of Genesis. As with Isaac, there are many types of Christ in the life of Joseph: (1) his father's love for him (Genesis 37:8-27; John 5:20); (2) the hatred of his brethren (Genesis 37:8-27; Matthew 27:1, 2, 22,23); (3) his temptation (Genesis 39:7-20; Matthew 4:1-11); (4) his promotion by Pharaoh (Genesis 41:40-44; Mark 16:19); (5) his marrying a Gentile bride during his rejection by his brethren (Genesis 42:50; Acts 15:14); (6) his revelation of himself to his brethren (Genesis 45:3; Zechariah 12:10).

A brief recap indicates the following outline which will help one to think through Genesis.

PRIMEVAL		PATRIARCHAL	
Chapters 1-11		Chapters 12-50	
(1) Creation	(chap. 1, 2)	(1) Abraham	(chap. 12-25)
(2) Fall	(chap. 3, 4)	(2) Isaac	(chap. 21-28)
(3) Flood	(chap. 5-9)	(3) Jacob	(chap. 25-36)
(4) Nations	(chap. 10, 11)	(4) Joseph	(chap. 37-50)

THE GOSPEL OF MATTHEW

The writers of the four Gospels all present Jesus, but each from a different viewpoint. None attempt a complete biography. They select incidents and discourses to emphasize the particular message to meet the needs of the people to whom they wrote. All wrote to all mankind, but each wrote primarily for a particular group.

Matthew intended his message primarily for the Jews. Mark wrote to a military people, the Romans. Luke presents Jesus as the perfect divine Man, addressing himself particularly to the Greeks, whose ideal was the perfect man; perfect morally, spiritually, and physically. John's testimony is given to prove that Jesus is the Christ, the Son of the living God, and is addressed to the Church in general.

Matthew presents Jesus to us as He is revealed in His words. His Gospel shows Christ to us through the Lord's speech, words, sayings, discourses, and doctrines. As Matthew writes he refers to and unfolds the significance of the past.

The purpose and the scope of the book are indicated in the first verse, "The book of the generation of Jesus Christ, the son of David, the son of Abraham." As the son of David, Jesus is shown as king; as the son of Abraham, He is obedient unto death. The word *kingdom* occurs 56 times, *kingdom of heaven,* 32 times, *son of David,* nine times.

The key idea is the word *fulfilled* or the phrase *that it might be fulfilled.* Matthew makes at least 60 references to the Old Testament writings as fulfilled in Christ.

Repeated readings of the Gospel of Matthew will bring truths to a person as stated above. These facts will help him get a bird's-eye view of the whole book. An outline of the book will develop in his mind. George Henderson, in *The Wonderful Word*, has given the following simple outline of Matthew's Gospel:

1. The Person of the King: chapters 1 to 4:16
   (a) His relation to *earth:* true, but sinless man; chapters 1 and 2.
   (b) His relation to *heaven:* beloved of the Father; chapter 3
   (c) His relation to *hell:* conqueror of the devil; chapter 4.
2. The Preaching of the King: chapters 4:17 to 16:20
   "From that time Jesus *began to preach"* (4:17).
3. The Passion of the King: chapter 16:21 to chapter 28
   "From that time forth began Jesus to show unto his disciples, how that he must . . . suffer . . . and be killed . . ." (16:21).

THE BOOK OF PHILIPPIANS

Philippians is the least systematic and doctrinal and the most warmly spontaneous and personally revealing of Paul's epistles. It is full of praise and thanksgiving. The note of joy predominates. "Rejoice in the Lord . . . Rejoice in the Lord always," (3:1; 4:4). The word *joy* in one form or another occurs 14 times. The epistle can be rightfully called the Joy Book.

The general theme may be summed up as "Christ is all." Each chapter has a key verse, thus giving us four main features of Christian life as follows:

Chapter 1. Christ our life: "For me to live is Christ" (1:21).
Chapter 2. Christ our example: "Let this mind be in you, which was also in Christ Jesus" (2:5).
Chapter 3. Christ our goal: "I press toward the mark for the prize of the high calling of God in Christ Jesus" (3:14).
Chapter 4. Christ our sufficiency: "I can do all things through Christ which strengtheneth me" (4:13).

Another birds's-eye view summarizes the Book under the idea of the joy of Christian life:

Joy in prayer (1:1-11)
Joy in suffering (1:12-30)
Joy in humility (2:1-11)
Joy in service (2:12-30)

Joy in knowing Christ (3:1-11)
Joy in spiritual growth (3:12-21)
Joy in the peace of God (4:1-9)
Joy in the strength of Christ (4:10-23)

Bible synthesis is meant to be more than an intellectual feast. If we approach the Bible with a proper attitude of prayer, we can expect to find great truths to enrich us spiritually, mentally, and physically.

THE BOOK OF EPHESIANS

Ephesians is the epistle of Church truth. When we open the epistle we enter the great cathedral of God, His temple in this present age. The doctrinal foundation for the cathedral is found in Romans. A description of the superstructure is found in Colossians, 1 Corinthians 12, and elsewhere. But in Ephesians the Holy Spirit through Paul gives us the most specific, the clearest, and the grandest revelations concerning this habitation for God in the Spirit—the Church or body of Jesus Christ.

Like most of Paul's letters, Ephesians divides naturally into two main sections. The first part deals with what a man believes, the latter portion takes up how a man behaves. And belief does determine behavior. The following is a brief outline of the epistle:

I. The call and design of the Church—the Church as God sees it: chapters 1 to 3.
  A. The conception of the Church: chapter 1.
    1. Planned by the Father: vv. 3-6.
    2. Provided by the Son: vv. 7-12.
    3. Wrought by the Holy Spirit: vv. 13, 14.
  B. The construction of the Church: chapter 2.
    1. His workmanship (literally, masterwork, masterpiece): v. 10.
    2. Christ is the chief cornerstone: v. 20.
    3. Built of living stones: vv. 19-22.
  C. The commission of the Church: chapter 3.
    1. God's purpose earthward: v. 9.
    2. God's purpose heavenward: vv. 10; 2:7.
II. The conduct and duty of the Church—the Church as God wants the world to see it: chapters 4-6.
  A. The character of the Church: chapter 4:1-16.

1. "One body . . . Spirit . . . Lord . . . faith . . . baptism . . . One God and Father . . . till we all come in the unity of the faith, and of the knowledge of the Son of God, unto a perfect man:" vv. 4-6, 13.

B. The conduct of the Church: chapters 4:17 to 6:9.
   1. Individual conduct: 4:17 to 5:21.
   2. Family conduct: 5:22 to 6:4.
   3. Employer-employee conduct: 6:5-9.

C. The conflict of the Church: chapter 6:10-24.
   1. The enemy defined: vv. 11, 12.
   2. The armor designated: vv. 10, 13-20.

6

Studying in Depth

ON THE SUBJECT OF INDUCTIVE STUDY Robert Traina states:
... induction is objective and impartial for it demands that one
first examine the particulars of the Scriptures and that one's conclusions be based on those particulars. Such an approach is sound
because, being objective, it corresponds to the objective nature of
the Scriptures. It produces hearers rather than speakers, and the
nature of the Scriptures requires hearers. Methodical Bible study,
then, is inductive Bible study, because in this instance induction is
methodical.[1]

In the inductive or direct method of study we carefully
examine a particular passage of Scripture for the purpose of
understanding its content, meaning, and application. This involves observation, interpretation, and application. To put it
another way, the student must discover what the author intended to say, recognize what he meant, and then receive his
message by submissiveness and obedience of spirit. We observe,
then conclude. This requires analysis that tells what a passage
actually had to say. At first we notice only that which is
obvious, but continued study will train us to discover deeper
truths.

Martin Anstey has written: "The true key to the understanding
of the Word of God is the sincere desire to ascertain just
exactly what the Spirit of God in the sacred writers intended
to convey. We must not take their words and read into them a
meaning of our own. We must receive the Word whether it
accords with our preconceptions or contradicts them." [2]

[1] *Op. cit.* [2] *How to Master the Bible* (London: Victory Press, 1931).

Bible analysis places emphasis upon the thread of truth. This thread can be found in a book, a chapter, a paragraph, even a verse. Finding the thread points up the essential unity of the Bible.

PROCEDURE IN INDUCTIVE STUDY

In literature, form or structure of the text is important. This is the key to be used in unlocking the contents. Any literary work is constructed around one main structural framework. Study reveals that the basic structure is made up of smaller units of composition. These are seen to be related to each other and to the whole.

The Bible is great literature and more. The application of the basic principle of literature is important in our study of the Bible. The Holy Spirit moved upon men of old to write words in the structural framework of this great Book which are meaningful in contributing to the whole. In other words, the writers did not record unrelated and aimless words. All was inspired of God and written with purpose.

The Holy Spirit directed each writer of Scripture to record only those things that needed to be said on a given subject; seldom, if ever, was everything included that could be said on a matter, whether it was a discourse, a biography, or historical record. The Bible does not claim to be a record of history, a text on science, or a code of ethics. Instead, the authors were inspired to select those things that would accomplish the purpose of their books. The material selected was arranged to suit that purpose.

The presentation of Christ by the writers of the four Gospels illustrates how each chose events and discourses from our Lord's life to develop the theme and purpose of his book. Matthew pointed his Gospel toward the Jews primarily. Mark wrote to the Romans who were a military people, and action leaps from its pages. Luke presents Jesus as the perfect divine Man, addressing himself to the Greeks, whose ideal was the perfect man. John wrote to prove that Jesus is the Christ, the Son of God, and addressed his Gospel to the Church in general.

Take a passage of Scripture for study. After reading it several times to discover the overall development, look for its main features. Is it prose or poetry, historical narrative or parable, expository teaching or prophecy? Next look for the major sections or units of thought.

To analyze a given passage properly and understand the intent and meaning of the author we must give attention to the content and form. All that God authors has order, form, and purpose. We need to discipline ourselves to see this picture in the Bible; it is insufficient to study some parts and bypass others. It is unwise to decide what the passage means until we are sure what it says.

Attention must be given to the laws that govern the composition of any good literature. This relates to structure and involves the parts that make up the whole and the relationship of these parts to one another. In other words, each segment, each chapter, each verse is interrelated to form one orderly and purposeful whole. No written Word of God is by happenstance and without purpose. Each small part—word, phrase, verse—can be identified with a truth which in turn relates to the main truth of the whole.

Remember that chapters and verses are not divinely inspired. We are grateful for the valuable work done by scholars a few hundred years ago to give us these identifications which greatly help us to locate or refer to a given passage. Bible study need not be confined to the divisions of chapter and verse. Keep this in mind when tempted to think of each verse as a separate thought. Try to fit verses into paragraphs. The paragraph is a logical division in presenting the development of a presentation of thought.

Three Steps

Next comes the spade work to lay bare the teaching of the passage. There are three steps built on a sequence of three questions. First is *observation*—what does it say or what do I see? The second is *interpretation*—what does it mean? The third is *application*—how does it apply to life? To me?

The first and the third tend to be neglected. It is essential to observe carefully what the passage actually says before interpreting, and then apply the message before moving on.

1. OBSERVATION: WHAT DOES THE PASSAGE SAY?

Two important techniques are involved; first, to make observations and, second, to ask questions. Observation has been described as the "art of seeing things as they are." Traina states, "The general function of observation is to enable one to become saturated with the particulars of a passage so that one is thoroughly conscious of their existence and of the need for their explanation. Observations supply the raw materials upon which the mind may operate in the interpretive process."

We must let the Scriptures speak for themselves. In our search to know God's truth we ask, "What does God say?" and, "How does He say it?"

Every Bible passage contains a principal truth. In addition to the primary meaning there often is a truth that is less obvious. A certain truth in a given portion may be very evident, while, on the other hand, there could be a less apparent gem to be dug out by the observing student. The Bible student has the task of ascertaining what God intended to say.

To correctly observe what the Bible says requires diligent application of five steps: (1) read, (2) record, (3) search, (4) relate, (5) recall.

Bible study begins and ends with reading. Paul urges, "Give attendance to reading" (1 Timothy 4:13). When beginning your observations, be sure to read the larger unit of Scripture first. Read the book as a whole before you study the chapters; the chapters before the paragraphs; the paragraphs before the verses; and the verses before the phrases and words.

The diligent student will make notes as he pursues his study. He will want to record his observations and be able to recall through meditation that which the Holy Spirit has made real to him. Someone has said that a pencil is the third eye for seeing Bible truth. The other two are the eye of the Holy Spirit and the physical eye. To study with pencil and notebook at hand cultivates the powers of observation, orderly thought, and memory. And always pray with the Psalmist, "Open thou mine eyes, that I may behold wondrous things out of thy law" (119:18).

The Holy Spirit has directed the Word of God to be written in such a manner as to challenge the student. The secrets of the Scriptures are as "silver" and "hid treasures" which are to be sought after (Proverbs 2:4). Jesus commanded us to "search the Scriptures" (John 5:39). Prayerful, diligent, sanctified effort is needed for this searching of the Word.

Kipling's famous lines are a good reminder to us:

> I have six trusty serving men,
>   They taught me all I knew;
> Their names are What? and Where? and When?
>   And How? and Why? and Who?

In observation you will ask: Where did the incident take place? Where did the people live who were involved? When did it occur in relation to other historical matters? To illustrate, Jesus came to this earth "when the fulness of time was come." Events, politically and otherwise, all contributed to preparing the world for His advent. You will also ask Who? Who wrote it? To whom? About whom? And then, What? What really happened? Let us pose two questions. Did the bears of 2 Kings in Elisha's day kill the 42 children? Did the angels sing the good tidings to the shepherds in Luke 2? Was it an apple which Eve ate in Eden to cause the Fall?

Take the healing of the leper (Mark 1:40-45). We look for and write down four things: (1) where (place); (2) who (persons); (3) what happened (events); (4) how or why (ideas). As we discuss the first two, we identify with these persons, their feelings, their outlook, their need. Item by item we ponder the list of events, asking key questions, and the answers give ideas. See the compassionate Christ, human in understanding, divine in His love and ability. See true faith, "thou canst make me clean"—no doubt there.

To find the meaning of a passage it must be related to other passages. The Scriptures never contradict themselves. Truth is many-sided. Both Paul and James draw their respective arguments regarding faith and works from the same Old Testament patriarch, Abraham. Paul writes of obedience in faith. James writes of obedience in action. They deal with complementary aspects of one truth. The better things of Christ as recorded in the Epistle to the Hebrews take on enriched meaning as we become acquainted with the tabernacle of Moses and the Old Testament offerings.

The record we keep of our observations is important. Whether or not the items that occur to us seem important or not, let us record them. The noting of minor details, seemingly insignificant at the time, may take on prominence as we begin to sift our observations.

Our notations might well include the following: (1) points, (2) problems (what does the passage say that I don't understand?), (3) parallels (what similar truths are found elsewhere in the Scriptures?), (4) precepts to obey, (5) promises to claim, (6) perils to avoid.

G. Campbell Morgan outlined four rules for this kind of study. He said, "Read and gain an impression. Think and gain an outline. Meditate and gain an analysis. Sweat and gain an understanding."

Correct observation is essential for correct interpretation. To know what the writer says puts us well on the road to understanding what he means.

2. INTERPRETATION: WHAT DOES THE PASSAGE MEAN?

After we have exhausted our observations, we proceed to answer the interpretive type of question "Why?" We list three:

1. "What does it mean?" This is the definitive phase of the investigation. The facts have been set forth and now the evidence is weighed in the light of all the rules of interpretation as covered in an earlier chapter. Additional tools can be used to profit. What do the words mean? The meaning of significant words can be discovered to unravel the meaning which can also bring rich blessing. For example, the Greek translated

"accepted" in Ephesians 1:6 appears one other time in the New Testament—in Luke 1:28 the angel Gabriel hails the virgin Mary with the words that she was "highly favored." We as God's accepted in Christ have been graciously accepted, much graced, highly favored.

2. "Why is this said?" This question searches for the occasion, the situation, and the historical setting. Tools that give light on Bible customs and manners will yield helpful information.

3. "What does this imply?" Here we seek for teaching. We seek to evaluate our findings in the light of other teaching as given in related passages. And we compare truth with truth, doctrine with doctrine. If there is only one mention of a particular truth in Scripture we do not hang doctrine and practice on it. To illustrate, no doctrine of proxy baptism can be deduced from 1 Corinthians 15:29.

Luther wrote that "the best teacher is the one who does not bring his meaning into the Scripture but brings it out of the Scripture." It is our task to determine the meaning of the Word of God, not to verify our presuppositions and prejudices; to discover the meaning, not to attribute one to it; to extract the meaning, not to import one into it.

The Parable of the Ten Virgins illustrates how Scripture can be interpreted through bias and prejudice. Arminians prove backsliding; Calvinists prove empty profession; entire sanctification people prove the second blessing; typologists make it teach pneumatology; some use it to prove that without the baptism in the Holy Spirit one is not ready for the coming of the Lord; eschatologists use it to set timetables. The oil in the vessels to some means readiness, but means repentance to others.

Some portions of Scripture are not easily understood. It is possible to grasp a Bible truth and yet never understand all the implications of that truth. But whatever we do, we must not be guilty of using verses as hooks upon which to hang doctrinal beliefs. For example, the mention of the word *water* in John 3:5 does not give license to teach baptismal regeneration. Passing references do not establish doctrine.

Essential truth is not veiled by obscure and incidental passages. Essentials are not hidden mysteries. Everything necessary to salvation and Christian living is set forth clearly.

When two interpretations can be proposed for a given Scripture portion, the clearest should be accepted. The clear passage should interpret the obscure; not the obscure, the clear. Doctrine is established by extensive references in the Word.

Men of different theological positions, often directly contradictory, assert the claim of Biblical authority for their positions. Catholics, Protestants, Calvinists, Arminians, evangelicals, liberals—all read the Scriptures differently. Incredible as it seems, even free love adherents, homosexuals, murderers quote some part of the Bible to justify their deeds. How do we explain this seeming confusion?

The answer is found in a twofold statement. All Scripture is inspired, but some parts are subject to illumination by other parts. For example:

1. The New Testament interprets the Old Testament. To place the Old Testament over the New is cultic. Religion is not summed up in the Ten Commandments. Worship is on the first day of the week, not the seventh. Christ supersedes the burnt offerings. We understand the Old Testament through the New.

2. The Epistles interpret the Gospels. The Gospels record the life and teachings of Christ. The Epistles systematize the doctrines. The Resurrection is recorded in the Gospels; its theology is developed in the Epistles.

3. The extensive teaching passages interpret those of incidental mention. Doctrinal subjects may be mentioned in isolated settings, but we find them explained in others. For example, justification is mentioned in Philippians and Titus, but the doctrine is set forth in Romans and Galatians.

4. The teaching passages interpret the symbolic and figurative. Figurative language has a large place in Scripture. Figurative elements are no less truthful than the plain and literal statements. They are used to teach eternal truths but must be

recognized for what they are. Doctrine is developed, however, upon the great extensive teaching passages.

One of the enriching experiences of Scripture study is the constant discovery of fresh truths. We will never exhaust the great riches of Bible content this side of eternity. When the writer finds a passage to be totally beyond his comprehension, he recognizes "the secret things belong unto the Lord our God: but those things which are revealed belong unto us and to our children for ever, that we may do all the words of this law" (Deuteronomy 29:29).

3. APPLICATION: HOW DOES THE PASSAGE APPLY TO ME?

The study of the Bible is not merely the learning of facts or unapplied doctrines. As the teaching of the Scriptures is discovered it must be put into practice. Every Scripture has one primary interpretation, but it may have many practical applications. "Doctrine personalized," states Irving Jensen, "is doctrine felt, and doctrine felt is doctrine applied."

The Bible says, "For whatsoever things were written aforetime were written for our learning, that we through patience and comfort of the Scriptures might have hope" (Romans 15:4). The Bible further states that the experiences of the children of Israel were for "our examples" (1 Corinthians 10:6, 11). The Bible is inspired and is "profitable for doctrine, for reproof, for correction, for instruction in righteousness: that the man of God may be perfect, thoroughly furnished unto all good works" (2 Timothy 3:16, 17).

We may know what God says and how He says it; we may know what the Bible says and what it means; but it only becomes of personal value when we make a personal application. Application is the purpose of the study of the Word of God. The application must not be made simply in thought. Either Christ is Lord and His Word our authority or they are not.

Applications are not interpretations and do not have the same status. A given passage has one meaning, but the moral principles may have many applications. Be sure, however, never to force the Scriptures to an unwarranted and farfetched application.

These are the questions to be answered if the Bible is to become relevant to life:

1. What does the Bible say (content)?

2. What does the Bible say to me (personal application)?

3. What does the Bible say to me today (relevant personal application)?

4. What am I going to do about it today (immediate personal action on God's Word to me)?

The will of the student is central to making Bible study relevant to life. J. H. Howett wrote, "Get a will behind the eye, and the eye becomes a searchlight, and the familiar is made to disclose undreamed-of treasure." We must will to study, and as we study we must will to obey.

If we do not assimilate and appropriate the truth of the Word, spiritual atrophy will result. The immediate purpose of Bible study is to reproduce the experience which in the first place produced the Bible. A Chinese student, having caught this basic principle, wrote, "I am now reading the Bible and behaving it." (See Mark 4:23-25.)

The Great Commission commands us to "disciple all nations" (Matthew 28:19). The mandate requires the student of the Word to go beyond observation, beyond interpretation, beyond personal application to his own life to the task of sharing the joys he has discovered in the Scriptures with others. The whole task is really not complete until the student has sought to communicate the truths that have been found. This is done by the minister sharing through preaching and teaching, by the teacher sharing in his teaching ministry to the class, and by the believer sharing in group Bible studies and personal witness.

7

Examples of Inductive Study

WE ARE NOW READY to examine a Bible passage. Let us recap some practical suggestions.

Approach the study hour with freshness of mind. Our best study is not done when we are weary mentally and physically.

Choose the passage. Read it over several times. Get a bird's-eye view of the whole, then explore the parts. Try to arrive at the intentions of the author. Find his purpose and note key words and expressions. What is each paragraph or unit of thought trying to say? Do paragraphs differ? How? What seems to be the thread of unity throughout? Search for this thread or chain. Connect the links of the chain.

Keep a record of all your observations, whether you think they are significant or not. After you have noted the words or phrases that seem to reflect the author's purpose and have found the thread of thought, you are ready to search for outside help on problem passages, look at parallel passages, and compare geography, history, and the like.

Through the entire process it is of the utmost importance to depend upon the Holy Spirit, without whom we cannot understand the Word of God.

EPHESIANS 1:1, 2

Observation supplies the raw materials upon which the Spirit-directed mind can work. Note these things in the first two verses of Ephesians:

1. Paul is the author.

75

2. He calls himself an apostle.

3. Paul further identifies himself as an apostle of Jesus Christ.

4. His apostleship is "by the will of God."

5. The letter is addressed to the "saints . . . at Ephesus, and to the faithful in Christ Jesus."

6. The mention of our Lord's name in the first instance is "Jesus Christ"; in the second it is "Christ Jesus."

7. The salutation is for "grace . . . and peace" to attend the recipients of the letter.

8. Grace and peace are to come from "God our Father, and from the Lord Jesus Christ."

9. God is acknowledged as our Heavenly Father.

10. The full name—the Lord Jesus Christ—of our Saviour is used. Each name is worthy of study, for it has special meaning.

11. Salutations as used by Paul are worthy of comparison and study.

The above are observations. The next step is to see if they are meaningful. They may provide a clew to our understanding of the passage.

This salutation in Ephesians is customary for Paul to use when addressing a letter to a church. Check all the letters to the churches. When he addresses a letter to a pastor, he adds a third word—mercy—to the salutation. See the letters to Timothy and Titus.

Words used include *apostle, will, saints, faithful, Ephesus,* and the names of Deity. The context in which these terms are used will help define their meaning.

Now, let us observe the structure of the passage. How do the terms fit into the literary unit? Is it a simple sentence? Compound? Complex? A simple declaration? A question? A command?

What is the mood communicated? Pleasure? Displeasure? Joy? Sadness ? Despair? Urgency? Determination? Tenderness? Apply the use of Kipling's "six trusty serving men"—what, where, when, how, why, who.

Interpretation hinges on the completeness and accuracy of observation. Application, which is the all-important goal, will fail if interpretation is not correct. For example, God's word to Hosea to take a harlot as his wife, or the Lord's command to Ezekiel to shave his head, do not mean that we are expected to do the same. We need to find out the what and the why. When these have been discovered, there may be a truth that can be drawn for application to us today, but not a custom to be followed.

Coming back to verses one and two of Ephesians 1, we pose at least three questions. The first interpretive question is What. For instance, What is an apostle? What is the will of God? Who are the saints? The faithful in Christ Jesus? Are they the same or two different groups?

A second question is Why. Answers will help us interpret. Does Paul always identify himself as an apostle? Why does he use the term in Ephesians? Why does he use two terms for the recipients?

A third interpretive question is the implicational one: What does the passage imply? To obtain our answer we make use of the laws of interpretation that relate to parallel passages and the existence of other Biblical facts. The use of other study tools will prove helpful. This may include concordances, Bible dictionaries, atlases, commentaries, and lexicons. Generally the concordance will be the most useful.

When we have brought our answers together our findings can be summarized. Then follows the important step which is the ultimate goal. This is to apply the passage to our own lives. Be specific. Avoid generalities. Many truths apply directly to life. Others are for "our example" in teaching a principle. For instance, God commanded Abraham to sacrifice Isaac. This passage must be limited to its historical context, but a timeless principle is found in it. God honors the man who obeys him. That is a principle changeless and timeless.

EPHESIANS 1:3-14

This passage—a paragraph—is one long sentence of 268 words in the Revised Version and three sentences totaling 268 words in the King James. The passage contains a volume of truths and doctrines vital to Christian faith and practice.

These three sentences (King James Version)—one paragraph—

bring a thread of truth regarding God's majestic plan of salvation. The thread can be noted in such phrases as: "in Christ" (v. 3); "in him" (v. 4); "before him" (v. 4); "in whom" (v. 7).

Look at the passage in this manner as related to God's work on our behalf past, present, and future.

Blessed be the God and Father of our Lord Jesus Christ, who hath blessed us with all spiritual blessings in heavenly places

(Past)	IN CHRIST:	(Present and future)
according as he hath chosen us	IN HIM	
before the foundation of the world,		that we should be holy and without blame in love:
	BEFORE HIM	
having predestinated us unto the adoption of children	BY JESUS CHRIST	to himself,
according to the good pleasure of his will, to the praise of the glory of his grace, wherein he hath made us accepted	IN THE BELOVED: IN WHOM THROUGH HIS BLOOD,	we have redemption the forgiveness of sins,
according to the riches of his grace; wherein he hath abounded toward us in all wisdom and prudence; having made known unto us the mystery of his will, according to his good pleasure which he hath purposed	IN HIMSELF:	that in the dispensation of the fulness of times he might

IN CHRIST,

gather together in one all things both which are in heaven, and which are on earth: even

IN HIM:
IN WHOM

also we have obtained an inheritance, being predestinated according to the purpose of him who

worketh all things after the counsel of his own will: that we should be the praise of his glory,

who first trusted

IN CHRIST.
IN WHOM

ye also trusted, after that ye heard the word of truth, the gospel of your salvation:
also after that ye believed, ye were sealed with that holy Spirit of promise,

IN WHOM

which is the earnest of our inheritance until the redemption of the purchased possession, unto the praise of his glory.

Paul launched into a subject—the song of salvation—so thrilling he could scarcely pause for breath. The first sentence has 89 words, the second 125, and the last 54.

God the Father planned redemption for us. In tribute to the Father (vv. 3-6) three of His acts on our behalf are mentioned: He *chose* us (v. 4); He *adopted* us (v. 5); He *accepted* us (v. 6). Acceptance is through the work and merit of the Beloved, His only begotten Son.

God the Son provided salvation for us. The second sentence of this passage pays tribute to the work of Christ (vv. 7-12). He *redeemed* us (v. 7); *He has made known the mystery of His will* (v. 9); *He has granted us an inheritance* (v. 11).

God the Holy Spirit has wrought salvation for us. He has given us: a *seal* (v. 13); an *earnest* of our inheritance (v. 14); a *pledge* of perfect redemption that will be ours at Christ's coming (v. 14).

Each of these three tributes to the Trinity ends with the same expression, *to the praise of his glory* (vv. 6, 12, 14). All God's purposes center in himself and are for His glory (Romans 11:33).

1 TIMOTHY 1:1-11

Using this basic truth, let us take a brief look at 1 Timothy 1:1-11. Much detail will be omitted for lack of space.

A simple, practical approach to study is suggested in 2 Timothy 3:16. Just as John 3:16 gives us the central verse of the Bible on how to become a Christian, 2 Timothy 3:16 gives us an important verse on how to grow as a Christian.

Any passage in the Bible—a verse, a chapter, a book—is God's Word and is profitable in four ways. Note them:

1. Doctrine, literally teaching. The Bible presents a system of truth containing all the knowledge of God, man, and the universe essential to spiritual growth. Find the teaching of the passage.

2. Reproof, which makes us feel keenly to what extent we have strayed from the divine standard.

3. Correction, meaning the Scripture is the plumb line by which we test the correctness of our thinking and the uprightness of our conduct. Some read the Bible to criticize and attempt to correct it. Blessing comes to those who read it for the purpose of allowing it to criticize and correct them.

4. Instruction in righteousness, meaning to apply the lessons learned in the passage to our personal life. As we compare our character and conduct with the precepts of the Scriptures, we are being practical about Bible study. Instruction is only effective to the extent that it is applied.

Remember Paul's statement: "All Scripture is given by inspiration of God, and is profitable for doctrine ... reproof ... correction ... instruction in righteousness" (2 Timothy 3:16).

In verses 1 and 2, which are a greeting, Paul is talking about Christian relationships—his own and that of his son in the faith—to the Lord. Verses 3 and 4 constitute a warning or charge to Timothy. Verses 5 through 11 set forth examples of violations of the warnings. All of these matters relate to teaching or doctrine. Next notice the reproof in verses 4 and 6-10 and the correction in verses 2 and 5. Make instruction in righteousness to be your personal application. Your analysis could be placed on paper as shown on page 83.

JOHN 11

As an example of inductive study, let us take a brief but incomplete look at a portion of John 11.

OBSERVATION	INTERPRETATION	APPLICATION
V. 1: "a certain man was sick, named Lazarus, ... Mary ... Martha"	Jesus fellowshiped with and was concerned about individuals—He was people-oriented.	Jesus has personal concern for people, for me, for my loved ones.
V. 2: " ... Mary ... anointed the Lord ...	This occurred later, possibly in gratitude (12:3).	God notes our expression of gratitude. Have I been faithful with my sacrificial offerings?
V. 3: "his sisters sent unto him ... he whom thou lovest is sick."	Mary and Martha had confidence in Jesus. They appealed to Him for help and spoke of Jesus' love for Lazarus.	Our first call, when in need, ought to be for the Lord's help. He loves us and wants to help us.
V. 4: "This sickness is not unto death, but for the glory of God ..."	Lazarus died (vv. 11, 21). But Jesus had not missed the mark for He looked to the final outcome and to God receiving glory.	We look at the now, the immediate. That's why we can't understand all that happens. But God does all things well. He sees the end from the beginning. We need to apply Rom. 8:28 to our circumstances.

V. 5: "Jesus loved Martha, and her sister and Lazarus."	Jesus' love is again underscored.	The Lord loves us.
Vv. 6, 7: "When he had heard therefore . . . abode two days . . . then . . ."	Two adverbs of time, when and then, speak to us. When Jesus heard the news, it was not time to go, but after two days it was time. The word therefore has meaning. It speaks of His divine timetable. He planned resurrection for Lazarus. No doubt Jesus in His humanity could have desired to rush to them because of His loving concern.	The Lord never arrives too late. Our place is to "trust . . . delight . . . commit . . . and rest" (Ps. 37:3-8).

Continuing observation and interpretation of the chapter can be highlighted by pointing out that:

Mary and Martha were alike in their disappointment (vv. 21, 32); but Mary was devoted, generous, sacrificial (vv. 2, 20), while Martha was practical and busy (20, 39; 12:2).

Apparently Jesus chose to speak to Martha concerning the resurrection (vv. 23-27) because her practical outlook caused her to lean more on reason than on faith. Her faith expressed in verse 22, shrivels in verse 24 and fades out in verse 39. Her faith was doctrinal assent to a distant event. Jesus wanted her to personalize it now.

Many other great truths come out of more detailed observation. The foregoing is listed as a partial example.

DOCTRINE (teaching)

  Christian relationships, verses 1,2

  Warnings, verses 3,4

    Examples of error, verses 5-11

REPROOF

  Avoid fables and endless genealogies, verse 4

  Avoid things the law forbids —

    murder, lying, defiling, verses 6-10

CORRECTION

  Grace, mercy, and peace from God, verse 2

  Love out of a pure heart, a good conscience,

    faith unfeigned, verse 5

INSTRUCTION IN RIGHTEOUSNESS

  How do I look at my relationship to God? To the brethren?

  Am I involved in thought, word, or deed with the

    items that come under reproof?

  What are the things that mar my influence

    for God?

  Do I really love out of a pure heart?

  What about my conscience?

  Do I have sincere faith?

  Is there a strain of hypocrisy

    in my life?

  What will I do to correct

    my failings?

8

Studying Topically

ONE VERY NATURAL APPROACH to the study of the Bible is the topical method. Here the goal is to discover what the Word teaches about any important subject. By the use of a good concordance this type of study approach becomes one of the easier methods. Topical study, however, goes beyond word study. Word study stays within the confines of the meaning of a particular word, whereas topical study takes in a general subject. It may refer to synonyms, anonyms, and even to references that are only implied in the passage. In this respect a tool beyond a concordance may prove helpful, such as *Nave's Topical Bible*.

We agree that it is important to know what great men have to say on important subjects. Millions listen to hear what the President or some leading authority has to say on some vital matter affecting our welfare. How much more important it is to hear what God has to say on subjects that have a bearing on us for all time and eternity. Far too many people know some things God has said—usually only a little bit—and so their knowledge is limited, and their ideas are imperfect. We can only know what God has to say on a given subject by going through the Bible and collecting the information on what He has said.

CAUTION FLAGS

Before proceeding further in developing the methods to be employed in topical studies, it might be well to raise some caution flags. We must guard against studying only those topics that appeal to us. Jesus said, "Search the Scriptures" (John 5:39), and this is not done if we give ourselves to the study of only certain portions. Jesus intended for us to study all Scripture (2 Timothy 3:16, 17). We tend to do those things that give us special delight and bypass those things that do not elicit as much interest. To maintain physical health we must nourish ourselves with a balanced diet. In like manner spiritual growth and health are maintained by a balanced spiritual diet. To illustrate, some people are so taken up with the study of prophecy they fail to have an interest in any other message of the Bible. The same could be said for other subjects.

Almost any Bible study group has some member who makes a nuisance of himself because he attempts to monopolize the time with a few pet subjects. Such a person lacks balance for, although he is well informed on his favorite topic, he is uninformed on many subjects of equal importance.

Further, far too often a doctrine is taught without proper understanding of all that the Bible teaches. The reprehensible error of many false cults is that they use only a few selected texts on a given topic. To avoid a lack of balance and accompanying doctrinal error we should make topical study systematic. Let it be comprehensive and cover more than just a casual treatment of certain items. The treatment should be comprehensive enough to cover the whole ground as recorded from Genesis through Revelation.

CLASSIFICATIONS OF TOPICS

Topical Bible study is often custom-made, for it may arise out of a situation or need. Current events give rise to keen interest on the part of both believers and unbelievers. Pentecostal circles have had burning issues to be settled doctrinally over the years. In the earlier part of the century the doctrine of the Trinity came under study. This led to the profound statement on the Adorable Godhead as found in the Statement of Fundamental Truths of the Assemblies of God. Current Arab-Israel relations as projected almost daily in the media awaken a desire to know what the Scriptures have to say. Other issues that create Bible study interest include the ecumenical stirrings, the charismatic outpourings in the old-line denominations, and similar gripping issues such as abortion and capital punishment. Here, again, care must be exercised not to get caught in the trap of majoring in minors and minoring in majors.

Topics of the Bible generally fall under the following classifications: (1) doctrines, (2) biographies, (3) events, (4) places, (5) duties, (6) words.

DOCTRINAL STUDY

Topical study of Christian doctrine is of great importance. Doctrinal truth is found in all the Bible. The more we study, the more we are amazed with the range of revealed truth. Doctrinal truth for the Church is found for the most part in the New Testament but is foreshadowed in the Old.

The study of doctrine is not reserved for theologians. Every Christian should study doctrine, for the entire structure of Christianity rests upon this foundation. Much of the church world is plagued with haziness of belief. Christians need clear-cut thinking regarding the basics on which God has dogmatically expressed himself in His Word. Jude exhorts, "that ye should earnestly contend for the faith which was once delivered unto the saints" (v. 3). Paul states the ministry gifts are given to perfect the Church, "That we henceforth be no more children, tossed to and fro, and carried about with every wind of doctrine, by the sleight of men, and cunning craftiness, whereby they lie in wait to deceive" (Ephesians 4:14).

Myer Pearlman stated, "Strong beliefs make for strong character; clear-cut beliefs make for clear-cut character. Of course, a person's doctrinal belief is not his religion any more than the backbone is the man's personality. But as a good backbone is an essential part of a man's body, so a definite system of belief is an essential part of a man's religion."

We need not be greatly concerned about creeds and dogmas,

but we must be concerned about doctrine which is the foundation of Christ's Church. Heresies would not gain such large
followings if believers were rooted and grounded in Christian
faith. Dogmas, human reasonings, and supernatural manifestations are correct only as long as they agree with the Word of
God. The Bible is the final authority.

Two Greek words, *didache* and *didaskalia,* are translated "doctrine" some 50 times in the New Testament. They bear the
meaning of teaching, the work of a teacher, and the thing
taught. Doctrine means teaching and can be either good or bad,
true or false.

The believer has a responsibility to understand the doctrines
of the Bible (Titus 2:7; 1 Timothy 4:6; Hebrews 13:9). Paul
emphasized the need of "sound doctrine" (1 Timothy 1:10;
2 Timothy 4:3; Titus 1:9); "sound words" (2 Timothy 1:13); being
"sound in the faith" (Titus 1:13); "wholesome words" (1 Timothy
6:3).

When a Topic Has Been Chosen

When a topic has been chosen, you will proceed to list all
the passages that relate to that subject. Thoroughness is important. Find all the Bible has to say on it. A good concordance,
a topical textbook, and margin references will be helpful. Unless
you take into consideration all Scripture, you can be guilty of
erroneous interpretation. Cultists usually create their theories
in this manner by quoting the Bible to prove their points,
but only through the use of isolated texts or by lifting verses
out of context.

To properly interpret you must be exact as well as thorough.
Carefully determine the exact meaning of the passage with
regard to the topic under study. Observe before you interpret.
Study the meaning and usage of words. The importance of
some words in Bible study lies not so much in their meaning
as in the relationships they indicate. It is also noteworthy that
some of the most important words of the Bible are simple,
commonly used connectives that act like flags to alert you to

God's truths. Greater attention will be given to the importance of the proper understanding of words later. A good Bible dictionary will be helpful.

Topical study procedure will further include examining passages in the light of parallel passages as well as words in comparison to parallel words. A study of context, parallels, and word meanings as a rule settles the meaning of a Scripture portion when it appears difficult. The difficult passage is often made plain by related passages.

Your basic procedure is similar for all types of topical study, whether it be related to doctrine, biography, event, place, duty, or a word. It is simply collection, organization, conclusions, and application. Usually you will have accumulated a large amount of material, but the mere accumulation of verses for the sake of thoroughness is not enough. The material must be organized. Verses should be chosen to make the subject clear and easily understood. Your result should be an analysis, combining sufficiency of details with clarity of meaning.

The aid of the Holy Spirit in your study can never be over-emphasized. Human searching and human intellect will not reveal divine truth. Searchers after truth have found human systems to be incomplete and without satisfaction. And the Lord has not promised that truth would come in its fullness in a moment. He did say, "If ye continue in my word, then are ye my disciples; and ye shall know the truth" (John 8:31). Jesus also said, "Thy word is truth" (John 17:17). The written Word reveals the living Word. All who come face-to-face with Him in personal relationship realize He is pure truth. The Holy Spirit comes to guide us into all truth (John 16:13).

You must never forget that the Word must be applied to you personally. It is not only a challenge to the mind; it is a cleansing agent to the heart. The object of your study is not really attained until the truth is applied in a manner to create a response. Bible truth must be translated into Christian living.

EXAMPLE OF THE DOCTRINE OF PRAYER

A. INSTANCES OF MENTION

1. The word *pray* occurs	292 times—225 times in the O.T.
	67 times in the N.T.
2. The word *prayed* occurs	65 times—31 times in the O.T.
	34 times in the N.T.
3. The word *prayer* occurs	114 times—83 times in the O.T.
	31 times in the N.T.
4. The word *prayers* occurs	24 times—2 times in the O.T.
	22 times in the N.T.
5. The word *prayest* occurs	2 times—both times in the N.T.
6. The word *prayeth* occurs	7 times—4 times in the O.T.
	3 times in the N.T.
7. The word *praying* occurs	20 times—6 times in the O.T.
	14 times in the N.T.

B. PRAYER DESCRIBED AS
1. Calling upon the name of the Lord (Genesis 12:8)
2. Crying unto God (Psalms 27:7; 34:6)
3. Drawing near to God (Psalm 73:28; Hebrews 10:22)
4. Looking up (Psalm 5:3)
5. Lifting up the soul (Psalm 25:1)
6. Lifting up the heart (Lamentations 3:41)
7. Pouring out the heart (Psalm 62:8)
8. Pouring out the soul (1 Samuel 1:15)
9. Crying to heaven (2 Chronicles 32:20)
10. Beseeching the Lord (Exodus 32:11)
11. Seeking unto God (Job 8:5)
12. Seeking the face of the Lord (Psalm 27:8)
13. Making supplication (Job 8:5; Jeremiah 36:7)

C. PRAYER DEFINED AS
1. Communion (1 John 1:3; 2 Corinthinans 3:18)
2. Supplication (Ephesians 6:18; Philippians 4:6)
3. Intercession (Romans 8:26, 27)
4. Consisting of adoration, thanksgiving (Philippians 4:6), confession (James 5:16; 1 John 1:9), petition (1 John 5:15)

D. PRAYER IS TO BE MADE
1. To God (Psalm 5:2)
2. In the name of Jesus (John 14:13, 14; 16:23, 24)
3. By the Holy Spirit (Romans 8:26, 27)

4. At all times
   a. Night and day (1 Timothy 5:5)
   b. Without ceasing (1 Thessalonians 5:17)
   c. Always (2 Thessalonians 1:11)
   d. Continuing instant (Romans 12:12)
5. Everywhere (1 Timothy 2:8)
6. Without hypocrisy and vain repetition (Matthew 6:5-7)
7. Fervently (James 5:16; Colossians 4:12)
8. In faith (Hebrews 11:1, 6; 1 John 5:14, 15; Matthew 21:22; James 1:6; Hebrews 10:22)
9. With submission to God (Luke 22:42)

E. POSTURE IN PRAYER
1. Standing (1 Kings 8:22; Mark 11:25)
2. Bowing down (Psalm 95:6)
3. Kneeling (2 Chronicles 6:13; Psalm 95:6; Luke 22:41; Acts 20:36)
4. Falling on the face (Numbers 16:22; Joshua 5:14; 1 Chronicles 21:16; Matthew 26:39)
5. Spreading forth the hands (Isaish 1:15; 2 Chronicles 6:13)
6. Lifting up the hands (Psalm 28:2; Lamentations 2:19; 1 Timothy 2:8)

F. ANSWERS TO PRAYER GRANTED
1. Immediately at times (Isaiah 65:24; Daniel 9:21-23)
2. Delayed at times (Luke 18:7)
3. Differently from our desires at times (2 Corinthians 12:8, 9)
4. Beyond our expectation (Jeremiah 33:3; Ephesians 3:20)

G. ANSWERS DENIED TO THOSE WHO
1. Regard iniquity in their heart (Psalm 66:18)
2. Live in sin (Isaiah 59:2; John 9:31)
3. Ask amiss (James 4:3)
4. Are wavering (James 1:6, 7)
5. Are self-righteous (Luke 18:10-14)

H. SUMMARY AND APPLICATION
1. Prayer, mentioned 522 times in the Bible, is very important.
2. Prayer is made to the Father in the name of Jesus.
3. We approach God with an attitude of worship, a sense of need, an assurance of faith, and submission to His will.

4. We need to draw nigh to God in prayer, placing ourselves at His disposal, so He might channel His creative faith through us.

Prayer implies the existence of God and the responsibility of man, and has no meaning for those who deny either. It is more natural that God in His great mercy should answer the prayers of His children, than that earthly parents should grant the requests of their children (Matthew 7:11).

BIOGRAPHICAL STUDY

People are fascinating. Human life is the most interesting fact in the world. Thought life centers on people. The human element is the center of appeal in every news story, in every daily event in life, and in every work of art. Abstract principles take on meaning as they relate to life and find expression in the thoughts and actions of persons. Ideals must come down to earth and breathe, talk, walk, and act in people to become useful and reasonable.

Marie Petrie writes in her book *Clues to Holy Writ* that the Bible is literature in its four most interesting forms. There are (1) Biographies—the word pictures of outstanding men; (2) Letters —the utterances of the heart; (3) Poetry—the loftiest thinking of men; and (4) History—philosophy exemplified.

The Bible is a book of fascinating biography. In proportion to its size, no book offers so large a collection of literature in which so many different persons—2,930 separate ones—appear as does the Bible. It is evident that God has chosen to give much of His Word in biographical form with divine purpose. When we live with Bible characters in their environments, observe their moods and passions, see their strengths and weaknesses, victories and failures, and recognize they are "subject to like passions as we are" (James 5:17), their lives become meaningful and helpful to us. The narratives are rich in devotional lessons and apply in everyday life. Basic principles are clearly set forth in a divine-human relationship.

Biblical biography not only provides profitable spiritual instruction for the believer; it also presents to him a very worthwhile manner of propagating Christian truth. Since everyone is interested in people and life and living things, educators have used the biographical method of teaching history, literature, and other courses with great success. The same method can be used effectively in teaching spiritual truth. Who among us did not thrill to the stories of Bible characters related to us in our childhood. Little girls love the stories of baby Moses in the ark and his sister Miriam, of Ruth, of Esther, the little boy Samuel, of Mary, and the Baby Jesus. And boys relive the stories of Daniel in the lions' den, David and Goliath, and scores of others.

The biographical method may be studied factually as biographical narrative, homiletically as narrative or character exposition, and polemically or apologetically as biographical argument.

BIOGRAPHICAL NARRATIVE

In biographical narrative, the aim is simply to learn the biographical facts concerning a Biblical personality, as those details are revealed either in a single book or in all Scripture.

BIOGRAPHICAL EXPOSITION

Biographical exposition is organizing the material in such a way that it can be logically presented in a preaching or teaching setting. This method of Bible study is quite devotional in nature and lends itself with greater appeal than biographical narrative.

In biographical-narrative exposition, the entire span of a man's life is considered with emphasis on God's dealings with him in the various events and developments of his life, as these dealings relate to him personally or to the history of a group or nation. The theme in this type is not so much the spiritual life of the person as it is God's care for His own or the preservation of God's chosen people. Biographical narrative exposition emphasizes events in the person's life, whereas character exposition emphasizes the qualities of an individual and only brings in events to illustrate the message. Character exposition deals more definitely with the character of a man and may involve only a single story relating to the man. Scripture provides enough material on some Biblical characters to permit either approach, but for many of them we are limited to one method of study.

LESSONS TO BE LEARNED

The records of the men of Scripture are helpful because they are complete transparencies. Every picture is painted realistically and offers valuable instruction. Most portraits are of good men; some are of wicked persons such as Jezebel, Judas, Naboth, Ahab, and Absalom. Good or bad, all are pictured objectively as warnings to us.

The Bible does not hide the fact that many of its greatest were subject to failure. None are so idealized that they become irrelevant to life as lived in their day or as we face it today. These men were of human clay and were not flawless. Scripture records the duplicity of Abraham, the upright man: the anger of Moses, the meek man; the weakness of Samson, the strong man; the fear of Elijah, the bold man; the carnality of David, the devoted man; the folly of Solomon, the wise man; and the failure of Peter, the rocklike man.

It is important to take into account God's true estimate of the men of the Bible. This will not lower them in our thinking; rather, it will magnify the grace of God and encourage us. Bible biographies have a spiritual value above all other biographies for they picture the reactions of the human nature to divine matters. They teach us to avoid similar pitfalls and to better adjust our lives to the will of God and harvest the great blessings of obedience to His will.

There is a further value in the study of Bible biographies. God has chosen to reveal His plan and purpose through representative men. We understand Genesis, the foundation book of the Bible, through God's dealings with ten representative men—Adam, Cain, Abel, Seth, Enoch, Noah, Abraham, Isaac, Jacob, and Joseph.

GUIDELINES TO FOLLOW

The following principles are offered as guides in biographical study:

1. Assemble all the references concerning the character to be studied, being certain not to confuse him with those bearing the same name.

2. Determine the meaning of the person's name; Bible names are meaningful.

3. Carefully study his background: his ancestry, his education, the environmental influences of his youth. Note these influences on men such as Moses, Paul, Peter, Timothy. Did they help him or hinder him?

4. Study his friends and associates.

5. Note the places where the person's life unfolds. Moses' life divides into three divisions of 40 years each: 40 years with royalty in Egypt, 40 years in Midian, and finally 40 years in leading Israel. Paul wrote great letters from prison.

6. Observe particular traits of character displayed by him in the varying situations of life.

7. List his strengths and weaknesses. What were the steps that led to his failures, faults, and shortcomings? How did they affect his future?

8. What was the great crisis of his life and how did he meet it?

9. What contribution did he make to his day and to ours?

10. What is the main lesson of his life, and what is its particular value to us?

EXAMPLE OF CHARACTER STUDY

W. G. Scroggie summarizes the biography of Jacob (Genesis 25:19 to 49:33) as follows:

1. The supplanter at Beersheba (well of the oath)—25:19 to 28:22.
   a. The birthright—25:19-34
   b. The blessing—27 and 28
      (1) The deceit of Rebekah and Jacob—27:1-29
      (2) The determination of Esau—27:30-45
      (3) The departure for Haran—27:46 to 28:22

2. The servant at Haran (very dry, or parched)—29:1 to 31:55.
   a. Jacob deceived—29:1 to 30:24
      (1) Jacob's contract—29:1-19
      (2) Jacob cheated—29:20-30
      (3) Jacob's children—29:31 to 30:24
   b. Jacob deceiving—30:25 to 31:55
      (1) Laban's cattle—30:25-43
      (2) Laban's charge—31:1-42
      (3) Laban's covenant—31:43-55
3. The saint at Hebron (fellowship)—32:1 to 45:28.
   a. Discipleship—32:1 to 33:20
      (1) The consternation of Jacob—32:1-21
      (2) The conflict at Peniel—32:22-32
      (3) The conciliation of Esau—chapter 33
   b. Discipline—34:1 to 45:28
      (1) In the dishonor done to Dinah—chapter 34
      (2) In the deaths of Rachel and Isaac—chapter 35
      (3) In the destruction (supposed) of Joseph—chapter 37
      (4) In the disgrace of Judah—chapter 38
      (5) In the departure of Benjamin—chapter 49
4. The seer in Egypt (land of depression)—46:1 to 49:33.
   a. Prophetic blessing on the two sons—chapter 48
   b. Prophetic blessing of the 12 sons—chapter 49

9

Appreciating the Old Testament

THE 66 BOOKS OF THE BIBLE are in two parts, the Old Testament and the New Testament. The books of the Old Testament divide into three classes: (1) historical: Genesis to Esther, (2) poetical: Job to Song of Solomon, and (3) prophetical: Isaiah to Malachi. The New Testament also divides into three classes: (1) historical: Matthew to Acts, (2) epistolary: Romans to Jude, and (3) prophetical: Revelation.

Christ is the central theme of Scripture and, as bearing on His person, the Old Testament is classified as preparation; the four Gospels as manifestation; the Acts as propagation; the Epistles as explanation; and the Revelation as consummation.

The Bible's message is complete. Every chapter and verse combines into perfect unity, and all parts are interdependent. To master any part one must really master the whole. For this reason one must not give disproportionate emphasis to certain portions.

The Bible is basically a theological book, but in relating the story of God's redemptive actions with men it repeatedly refers to historical situations involving specific persons, places, and times. It is agreed that the New Testament is the mountain-top of God's written revelation. Without qualification, it is the most important single book in the world. The New Testament is the final, complete, and clear explanation of the provisions of God's great plan of redemption.

The importance of the New Testament, however, in no wise

diminishes the importance of the Old Testament. The writers of the New Testament claim that the story of Jesus Christ is rooted in history and not in "cunningly devised fables" (2 Peter 1:16). This historical consciousness is also characterized in the writings of the Old Testament.

MANY DISREGARD THE OLD TESTAMENT

The early books of the Bible present a series of pictures to which reference and explanation are made in the New Testament. Regrettably many people read the New Testament without any reference to or understanding of the Old Testament. Some even look upon the Old Testament as being made obsolete and impractical by the coming of the New Testament. But the Old Testament lays the foundation, plants the seed, and makes the needed preparation for all that appears in the New Testament. Augustine put it in sharp focus:

> The New is in the Old contained;
> The Old is in the New explained.

The Old Testament provides us with an account of God's movements in history to redeem sinful men. It provides a basis for understanding the life, death, and resurrection of Jesus Christ, who came to save us from our sins and provide us fellowship with God. Unbelievers are shown the way to God, and believers are shown how to walk with God. Writing of the Old Testament (for that was Scripture at the time of Timothy's childhood), Paul told Timothy that "the holy Scriptures" were able to make him "wise unto salvation" (2 Timothy 3:15). That was the way to God. Timothy was further reminded that "All Scripture is given . . . that the man of God may be perfect, thoroughly furnished unto all good works" (vv. 16, 17). In other words, the Old Testament (the Scripture of Timothy's childhood) was also able to show one how to walk with God.

BOTH TESTAMENTS NECESSARY

No one can ever understand the full scope of God's revelation without knowing the relationship between the Old Testament and the New Testament. Each needs the other. The Old Testament is God's covenant with man before the coming of the Lord Jesus into the world. The New Testament is God's covenant with man, through His Son, the Lord Jesus Christ. The eternal living Word, the Second Person of the Trinity, is the central Person of the entire Bible. The Old Testament looks forward to Him; the New reveals Him.

THE OLD TESTAMENT IS INCOMPLETE

Every word, every part, every book of the Bible is perfect because it is the Word of God. But the Old Testament by itself, as lengthy as it is and marvelous as it is in unity and purpose, is incomplete. It points toward the Redeemer promised at the time of the Fall. From Genesis to Malachi it is a Book of promise, one that looks forward to fulfillment. The Old Testament awaited "the fulness of time" when God was to send "forth his Son, made of a woman, made under the law, to redeem them that were under the law, that we might receive the adoption of sons" (Galatians 4:4, 5).

THE OLD TESTAMENT IS IMPORTANT

The massive testimony of the New Testament to the importance of the Old must be noted as significant. About one-tenth of the New Testament is really Old Testament material. This same ratio holds with respect to the recorded words of Jesus. There are at least 295 separate and specific references to the Old Testament in the New Testament, and they are found in 352 verses. Of 278 different Old Testament verses referred to in the New, 94 are from the Pentateuch, 99 from the Prophets, and 85 from the Writings.

Jesus quoted the Old Testament as the very words of God. A striking means by which to study how Jesus used Old Testament Scripture is to read through the Gospels of Matthew and John, making a careful note of each of His references to "the law" or to "the Scriptures." He appealed to almost every main section of the Old Testament. For example, in a threatening situation recorded in John 10:34-36 the Lord based His argument on one word in Psalm 82:6. In His application Jesus collectively referred to Scripture as "the law"—the entire Old Testament—as binding upon His hearers and then states emphatically "the Scripture cannot be broken." Recall the occasion when the Sadducees were discussing the wife who had been married to seven brothers successively. In answer to their question, "In the resurrection whose wife shall she be?" Jesus quoted Moses as "spoken unto you by God" (Matthew 22:23-33; Exodus 3:6). Some other examples are Matthew 26:31, a citation from Zechariah 13:7; Mark 14:49; John 13:18, a citation from Psalm 41:9.

Examples of claiming the statements of Old Testament writers as the Word of God are found in Hebrews 3:7, where the words of David (Psalm 95:7-11) are quoted "as the Holy Ghost saith"; in Hebrews 9:8, where Jeremiah 31:34 is cited, ". . . the Holy Ghost also is a witness to us . . ."; and Acts 28:25, where Paul attributes a quotation from Isaiah 6:9, 10 to the Holy Spirit by stating, "Well spake the Holy Ghost by Esaias the prophet."

An Overview of the Old Testament

I. History—17 books
A. The Pentateuch—5 books
    1. Genesis: ruin through the sin of man.
    2. Exodus: redemption through the blood of the lamb.
    3. Leviticus: communion through atonement.
    4. Numbers: direction through the pillar of cloud and fire.
    5. Deuteronomy: destination with instruction.
B. The Historical Books—12 books
    1. The Pre-exile Books
        a. Joshua: possession by entering (1-5), overcoming (6-12), and occupying (13-24).
        b. Judges: declension with six apostasies and servitudes, with divine interventions.
        c. First Samuel: transition from theocracy to monarchy.
        d. Second Samuel: confirmation of David on the throne.
        e. First Kings: disruption of the nation into two kingdoms.
        f. Second Kings: dispersion from which only a "remnant" of Judah returned and none of Israel did.
        g. and h. First and Second Chronicles: recapitulation of the Kings. The latter reviewed the disaster from the viewpoint

of the throne, the Chronicles from the viewpoint of the temple.
2. The Post-exile Books
    a. Ezra: restoration as a remnant return.
    b. Nehemiah: reconstruction of the walls of Jerusalem.
    c. Esther: preservation.

II. THE POETICAL BOOKS—5 books
A. Job: blessing through suffering.
B. Psalms: praising through praying.
C. Proverbs: prudence through precept.
D. Ecclesiastes: verity through vanity.
E. Song of Solomon: blessedness in communion.

III. THE PROPHETICAL BOOKS—17 books
A. The Major Prophets—5 books
    1. The Pre-exile Prophets
        a. Isaiah: the God who rules all history.
        b. Jeremiah: the God who avenges sin.
    2. Lamentation: clouds with a rainbow.
    3. The Post-exile Prophets
        a. Ezekiel: the God who overrules all.
        b. Daniel: the God who plans the future.
B. The Minor Prophets—12 books
    1. The Pre-exile Minor Prophets—9 books
        a. Hosea: the God whose love is always there.
        b. Joel: the God who appeals before punishing.
        c. Amos: the God who can no longer withhold judgment.
        d. Obadiah: the God who judges rightly.
        e. Jonah: the God who spares the repentant.
        f. Micah: the God who chastises to bless.
        g. Nahum: the God who cannot be mocked.
        h. Habakkuk: the God who justifies.
        i. Zephaniah: the God who punishes abused privilege.
    2. The Post-exile Prophets—3 books
        a. Haggai: the God who restores lost blessing.
        b. Zechariah: the God who brings new mercies.
        c. Malachi: the God who appeals to prove Him.

NEW TESTAMENT INTERPRETATION OF THE OLD

The New Testament offers a strikingly illuminating interpretation of the Old Testament. The examples given in the Old Testament are an important clew to correct interpretation of the Bible. Jesus and the apostles taught that the complete meaning of certain Old Testament texts would be effected in the redemptive revelation connected with the incarnation and mediatorial ministry of Christ. Note four key terms:

1. *Fulfill*, which appears over 30 times in the New Testament, such as in Matthew 1:22; 5:17. In other words, the event in the New Testament was a fulfillment of that which was either only partially disclosed or merely announced in the Old Testament.

2. *True or truth*, implying a contrast with the incomplete or partial disclosure. Examples are John 1:17; 6:32.

3. *Type* (Romans 5:14; 1 Corinthians 10:6) and Antitype (Hebrews 9:24; 1 Peter 3:21), with the emphasis upon one pattern of truth with various historical manifestations.

4. *Shadow* (Colossians 2:17; Hebrews 8:5; 10:1).

Study by Types

Large portions of the Old Testament become meaningful as we understand their typical meaning. Exodus and Leviticus open to those who see their intent and purpose as revealed in the antitypes of the New Testament. The writers of the New Testament interpret the Old Testament by explaining its types. Modernists may object to the study of types in the light of their rejection of the Old Testament as anything but an old storybook of the Jews, but type study opens new vistas of Bible truth to earnest students.

What Is a Type

The word *type* does not appear in the English Bible with the exception of a marginal reference on 1 Corinthians 10:11, where the word translated "ensamples" is shown to mean types. On the other hand, the word *tupos*, from which we get our word *type*, occurs 16 times in the New Testament. For example, it is rendered "print" (John 20:25), "example" (Hebrews 8:4, 5), "pattern" (Titus 2:7), "shadow" (Colossians 2:16, 17), "sign" (Matthew 12:39), "figure" (Hebrews 11:19), "allegory" (Galatians 4:24), "seal" (Romans 4:11), "letter" (2 Corinthians 3:6). Literally it means "stamp" or "impress."

Eight words are used to set forth the antitype or reality to which the type corresponds. They are: "figure" (1 Peter 3:21), "body" (Colossians 2:17), "very image" (Hebrews 10:1), "good things to come" (Hebrews 10:1), "things in the heavens" (Hebrews 9:23), "the true" (Hebrews 9:24), "the spirit" (2 Corinthians 3:6), "spiritually" (Revelation 11:8).

Possibly the best definition of the word *type* is given by Paul in his letter to the Colossians, "a shadow of things to come" (Colossians 2:17; compare Hebrews 10:1). A type is a God-ordained means of communicating truth in illustrative form. In other words, behind the historical interpretation of the Scriptures where the word or series of words is used, there lies the spiritual. The brazen serpent on a pole (Numbers 21:9) is a part of the historical record during Israel's wanderings, but it presents, in type, the death of Jesus.

To say that one thing is a type of another requires more than mere resemblance. Not only must the former resemble the latter; it must be designed to resemble it. This then becomes the relationship of the type and the antitype. Antitype literally means "answering the type."

A type involves three things: (1) an outward object or thing that represents a higher thing; (2) the higher thing, which is called the antitype or the reality; (3) the work of the type, which the Bible calls a "shadow." A type is a sign, an example, a pattern, a figure. A parable is an earthly story with a heavenly meaning; a type is a visible, earthly thing which the Lord has designed to teach us an invisible, heavenly, or spiritual thing. The type is the shadow; the antitype is the substance.

The study of typology is closely associated with the study of prophecy. Almost every type has something of a prophetic nature. A type prefigures a coming reality, while prophecy foretells it. Typology and prophecy, while holding marked similarities, are separate methods of setting forth truth. Typology uses representative persons, places, institutions, and symbols, whereas prophecy uses figurative language.

Types, generally, relate to redemption, either as to the person and work of Christ, or to the believer. Some relate to the Holy Spirit and the Church.

The Pentateuch contains most of the types. Some are in the historical books, and few, if any, are to be found in the poetical and prophetical books. This is to be expected. The great truths of redemption must needs be set forth in the early books, but as the revelation of redemption proceeds, types give way to the spoken word of the prophets. The great typical teachings became the basis for the flaming ministry of the prophets, for they spoke of a redemption to come.

WHY STUDY TYPES

In 1 Corinthians 10:11 we are told concerning the wilderness experiences of the Israelites that "all these things happened unto them for ensamples [types]." Paul explains that the record of these events is given to us for the purpose of teaching us lessons. This would include the events from the deliverance out of Egyptian bondage to the time of coming into the land of promise. These were actual events, but they had deep spiritual meaning for New Testament saints.

Typology must be studied within the boundaries of certain principles. It is scriptural to study this subject, for the writers of Scripture and the Lord himself made so many references that used types for teaching great lessons. As the surgeon's knife is of greatest value in the hands of the surgeon, so the Bible is most effectively used by those who are skilled in its interpretation. Those who wish to explore the great spiritual applications of the Pentateuch and other portions of the Old Testament will find a study of types to be almost a must to accomplish such an end. The Holy Spirit uses the things that are seen to illumine and teach us the things that are unseen.

The Old Testament types were for the purpose of illustrating or throwing light on the great precepts and doctrines revealed in the New Testament. The type is insufficient in itself, but it throws light on the gem of New Testament truth, causing the light to shine into our minds as the Holy Spirit makes application to our spiritual intelligence.

Types were given for the purpose of manifesting that which pertained to the Law of Moses, preparing the way for the fuller and better things in the antitype. All that pertained to the old covenant was but temporary as a forerunner or preparation for the better things in the new covenant. Every type is but the shadow of which antitype is the substance.

The study of types is important for:

1. The Holy Spirit placed them in Scripture (Exodus 26:33; Mark 15:38; Hebrews 9:6-9; 10:19-22).

2. Jesus himself constantly referred to them. Take note of the Gospel of John alone: John 1:14: the antitype of the tabernacle; 1:29: the fulfillment of the Old Testament sacrifices; Christ compares himself, 2:19: to the temple; 3:14: to the brazen serpent; 6:31-35: to the manna; 10:11: as the antitype of the Old Testament shepherds; 12:24: as the corn of wheat that brought forth the sheaf of the firstfruits; 13:10: as the laver; 15:1: as the true Vine; chapter 17: as the Great High Priest.

3. Paul declares that Israel's experiences in the wilderness, covering a lengthy portion of Scripture, "happened unto them for ensamples [types]" (1 Corinthians 10:11).

4. Typology is another evidence of the essential unity of the Bible. The two Testaments are united in relating the great plan of redemption. Both must be the product of the same mind, for they are intertwined in one great plan to present the eternal purpose of God.

RULES GOVERNING TYPES

Some have taken the study of types far beyond the realm of sensible interpretation. This area of study can be very helpful, but it demands mental restraint and controlled imagination. Lacking these, one becomes open to fanaticism.

There are rules that govern the study of types. The writers of Holy Writ never destroyed the historical sense of Scripture to establish the spiritual. Bear in mind that doctrines are not built on types. Our doctrinal beliefs are founded on the statements of God's Word and are illustrated by types. We cannot arbitrarily set something forth as a type merely because of resemblance.

The Bible clearly defines many types. For example, the "law having a shadow of good things to come" (Hebrews 10:1); "Adam . . . who is the figure of him that was to come" (Romans 5:14); Canaan is pictured as a figure of "a better country, that is, an heavenly" (Hebrews 11:16); the tabernacle of Moses with its priesthood, offerings, and furnishings is set forth as a figure of great typical teaching (Hebrews 9:8-11).

The Bible indicates other types by an interchange of names between the type and the antitype. As illustrations, note that Christ is called "the last Adam" (1 Corinthians 15:45), or "the Lamb of God" (John 1:29), or "our passover" (1 Corinthians 5:7).

Another warrant for a type is found where an evident analogy exists between some Old Testament event, person, or object, and the spiritual truth to which it points in the New Testament. Examples include Joseph as a type of Christ, Jonah and the whale illustrating the death, burial, and resurrection of Christ, and Israel's experiences from Egypt to Canaan as a type of the Christian's life.

The Passover is a type of the Lord's Supper. Circumcision is a type of baptism. Leprosy is a type of sin and its pollution. Hagar and Ishmael are types of the covenant of works.

A last and very important rule for types is to recognize that, as there is similitude between the type and the antitype, there is also dissimilitude. We fall into error when we try to make details typical. Adam was a type of Christ, but the last Adam infinitely surpassed the first Adam. Jonah was a type of Christ in the one experience of being in the fish for three days. No type is total.

KINDS OF TYPES

There are several helpful ways of grouping types. Someone has said that Genesis has the dispensational types, Exodus the redemption types, Leviticus the sacrificial types, Numbers the wilderness types, Joshua the Canaan types, the Historical Books the kingdom types, and the Prophets the prophetic types. All types fall into three general groups: (1) persons, (2) ceremonies, and (3) historical.

A. PERSONS

1. Adam: a type of Christ (Romans 5:14)
   a. As head of creation (Genesis 1:26; 2:19, 20; Psalm 8:3-6; Hebrews 2:5-9).
   b. As head of the race: the first Adam of the fallen race, the last Adam of the redeemed (Romans 5:12, 17).
   c. As head over Eve (Genesis 2:21-24; Ephesians 5:25-32). The first Adam and his wife were one flesh (Genesis 2:24); the last Adam and His bride are one spirit (1 Corinthians 6:17).

2. Abel: his blood cried for vengeance (Genesis 4:10); Christ's blood speaks for pardon (Hebrews 12:24).

3. Enoch: a type of the saints who are to be translated (Genesis 5:24; Hebrews 11:5; 1 Thessalonians 4:14-17).

4. Noah: a type of the Jewish people, left on earth but preserved through the Great Tribulation (Genesis 6:9; Jeremiah 30:5-9; Revelation 12:13-16).

5. Melchizedek: a type of Christ the King-priest (Genesis 14:18; Hebrews 6:20; 7:1-4, 23, 24).

6. Isaac: a type of Christ "obedient unto death" (Genesis 22:1-10; Philippians 2:5-8) and of Christ as the Bridegroom of a called-out Bride (Genesis 24).

7. Moses: a type of Christ as Prophet (Deuteronomy 18:15-19; Acts 3:19-23).

8. Aaron: a type of Christ as Priest (Exodus 28:1; Hebrews 2:17; 5:1-5).

9. David: a type of Christ as King (Isaiah 55:3; Acts 13:26-37).

10. Jonah: a type of Christ's death, burial, and resurrection (Jonah 1:17; Matthew 12:39-41).

Abraham typifies many characteristics of the fatherhood of God. Jacob illustrates the special leading of God, and Joseph presents a full picture of Christ as the Beloved of the Father. Elijah is a type of John the Baptist. In many points, Joshua, Samson, Solomon, Elisha, Zerubbabel, and Joshua, the high priest, are types of Christ.

Numerous groups or orders of persons are types. Among these are the Nazarites, the Jewish nation, the "firstborn," the prophets, priests, and the kings.

B. CEREMONIES

1. The Passover (Exodus 12; John 19:32-36; 1 Corinthians 5:7; 1 Peter 1:18, 19).

2. The tabernacle (Hebrews 9:1-28). The Books of Exodus and Leviticus abound with types found in the tabernacle and offerings. Great doctrines are typified in the furnishings of the tabernacle (Exodus 25 to 40). Incarnation is illustrated in the veil; justification at the altar; sanctification at the laver; intercession at the golden altar; worship in the holy of holies; communion at the table; reconciliation at the mercy seat. The table of shewbread, the ark of the covenant, the golden candlesticks are types. Among the many other ceremonial types are the offerings: the burnt offering, the sweet savor offering, the meal offering, the peace offering, the sin offering, and the trespass offering. These are rich with spiritual truths as they portray the atoning work of the Lord Jesus Christ (Leviticus 1 to 7).

3. Other significant types are portrayed by the consecration of the priests (Exodus 28, 29; Leviticus 8, 9), the cleansing of the leper (Leviticus 13, 14). Ceremonial acts such as circumcision and the laws of purification are typical. Then there are the festivals (Leviticus 23): (a) the feast of the Passover showing forth redemption; (b) the Feast of Unleavened Bread, a holy walk; (c) the Feast of Firstfruits, resurrection; (d) the Feast of Pentecost, the outpouring of the Holy Spirit; (c) the Feast of Trumpets, symbols of testimony; (f) the Day of Atonement; (g) the Feast of Tabernacles, both a memorial and prophetic feast like the Lord's Supper. Other ceremonial types include the sabbaths (seventh day and seventh year) and the year of jubilee (Leviticus 25).

C. HISTORICAL

The miraculous experiences of the children of Israel in their journey from Egypt to Canaan are specifically declared to be types (1 Corinthians 10:11) of the believer from the time he comes under the protection of the sprinkled blood until he enters into the promised rest (Hebrews 3:7 to 4:11). The most prominent types are:

1. The Passover: redemption by blood (Exodus 12; Ephesians 1:7).

2. The Red Sea: leaving the world behind (Exodus 14; Galatians 1:4; 6:14).

3. The tabernacle: access to God (Exodus 25; Hebrews 10).

4. Manna and water: provision (Exodus 16, 17; John 6, 7).

5. Perils: a grumbling and critical spirit (Numbers 20:3), unbelief (Exodus 13, 14), backsliding (Numbers 14:4), compromise (Joshua 9).

6. Victory through faith in God and obedience to His Word (Joshua 1).

Other historical places and incidents, rich in typical meaning, include the burning bush (Exodus 3; Acts 7:30), Mount Sinai, and the cities of refuge (Joshua 20). This is but a partial list.

10

Studying Smaller Units

THE ORIGINAL TEXT OF THE BIBLE had no chapter and verse divisions. Chapter divisions were made about A.D. 1250, and verse divisions were made many years later. The work of Cardinal Hugo in dividing the Scriptures into chapters, and that of Athias dividing the Old Testament into verses and Robert Stevens doing the same for the New Testament, has been of great value to Bible readers for purposes of identification.

But chapter divisions are often imperfect and break units of thought. For example, the great 53rd chapter of Isaiah on the humiliation and glorification of Christ should really begin at Isaiah 52:13. The same can be said of several other verse divisions. The student should always keep this fact in mind and watch for proper paragraph divisions.

Dr. Charles E. Fuller declared, "Three basic steps are to be carried out: (1) The smallest thought-units (independent clauses and sentences) must be understood first of all, (2) the relationship between successive clauses must be grasped, usually by noting the connectives that introduce each clause, and (3) we must seek to determine the function or the relationship between the larger thought-units until an entire book is seen as composed of successively larger units."

CHAPTER STUDIES

Despite the imperfection that may exist with respect to chapter divisions, this type of study may be one of the most common of all.

When studying a book of the Bible, first read the book through carefully, attempting to grasp the general idea. Next read the book chapter by chapter. Use a note pad to jot down the main subject. Some chapters may have two or more general themes. Follow this by a paragraph study of the chapter. Paragraphs are found by locating the topic sentence.

The following will help in chapter study:

1. *Main subject.* Most chapters have a chain of development bringing into focus the main truth. To find the chain we look for the links. The chapter must be studied until the main subject is discovered. On this matter Wilbur M. Smith has some helpful suggestions:

If a chapter does not have at least one great truth for us upon our first reading of it, then we ought to read it over again. If the time has gone for our devotional reading on any one day before the chapter has yielded some truth for our souls, then we can give it further thought while . . . (en route) to work, or as we go about the house in the normal duties of every day; and often by nighttime we will find the chapter yielding some rich truths for our souls. If necessary, go back to the chapter the next day, or take the next chapter for a change and then go back to the earlier chapter a day or so afterwards, but do not let that particular passage in the Word remain for you a barren area: keep drilling through the soil and rock until you strike the Living Water. My own experience has been that a chapter which involved the most thought, and which at first refused to give me anything, finally yielded up some spiritual teaching of unusual riches.

2. *Prominent persons.* Give attention to each one. Use a concordance to trace other references to him. Rich truths can be developed by comparing other references relating to some lesser known person.

3. *Key verse.* Look for the main verse, a key to the chain of truth in the chapter.

4. *Other points.* Observe the commands to obey, the promises to claim, the lessons to learn, the errors to avoid, the prayers to pattern after. Relate the chapter to the entire book and to Christ

and His redemption, which is the great theme of Scripture. Watch for key expressions and words.

5. *Summary.* Keep three general rules in focus: (1) relate the chapter to its context, (2) find the links in its chain of development, and (3) make personal application of the truths discovered.

VERSE STUDIES

Where is the Christian who has not been richly blessed by meditation on a single Bible verse? How often have you found the needed strength for the day or for a difficult trial as a verse leaped from the pages of Scripture and brought the needed faith, strength, or comfort for the hour?

Scores of personal experiences could be shared. During a time of undergoing deep concern over a great doctrinal crisis among the churches of our Movement years ago, and then on a given night after a trying business meeting involving a tragic local church situation, I arrived home about three in the morning a totally exhausted district superintendent. The burden was one far beyond mere physical exhaustion. Sleep fled from me, and body, mind, and spirit had almost reached the end of strength to carry on. At that point the Heavenly Father dropped a nugget in a tired mind and heart. Out of the blue came His assuring word, "When the enemy shall come in like a flood, the Spirit of the Lord shall lift up a standard against him" (Isaiah 59:19). There was the answer—simple, reassuring, faith-giving, uplifting, complete. Rest came immediately. True, the doctrinal problem of the churches and the problem of the local church still existed, but they were no longer a problem in my spirit. And, thank God, those issues were soon settled. Other situations too numerous to mention could be shared. A verse gave faith for remarkable healing—another at a time of decision making, and on and on.

When learning a verse meditate upon it; analyze it; take it apart and put it together again. Study the verse in relation to its context, then find the chain of thought.

The key to the understanding of any sentence lies in understanding the verbs. To understand the intent of the author, let us ask what the sentence does, or what does it demand to be done. The spiritual meaning rests upon the exact force of the leading word or words.

For example, see the lesson of letting verbs speak as recorded in Psalm 119:7-16. For the sake of having the usual construction of a simple English sentence, liberty has been taken in rewording the sentences. Focus attention on the expressions *I have* and *I will*. If we do these things expressed in the present perfect tense (I have), we can experience those listed in the future tense (I will). There are four "I haves" and six "I wills."

(Because) I have sought thee (v. 10),
             I will praise thee (v. 7).
(Because) I have hid thy word (v. 11),
             I will keep thy statutes (v. 8);
             I will meditate in thy precepts (v. 15).
(Because) I have declared thy judgments (v. 13),
             I will delight myself in thy statutes (v. 16)
             I will not forget thy word (v. 16).
(Because) I have rejoiced in the way of thy testimonies (v. 14),
             I will have respect unto thy ways (v. 15).

WORD STUDIES

Bible study always brings interest in words. Always bear in mind that the very words in Scripture are divinely inspired, not merely the thoughts. Every word in the original text is God-breathed. Correct understanding of the Bible comes through correct understanding of the words it uses. The understanding of a passage often depends upon the understanding of a single word. For example, take Isaiah 6:9: "For unto us a child is born, unto us a son is given." Accuracy is complete. The Child was born, but the Son was never born. He was the eternal Son, but was born in Bethlehem's manger as the Child in His incarnation.

When you come across a word in the Bible that you don't understand, you can do two things. The first is to look it up in a dictionary, particularly a Bible dictionary. But this may not solve your problem. For instance, the dictionary may give several meanings for the word, and you will still have to decide which one applies in the particular case. Your concordance and a book such as *An Expository Dictionary of New Testament Words*, by W. E. Vine, will be helpful.

The second thing you can do is to read the context, that is the sentences before and after it to see whether the writer indicates the meaning by the way it fits into the whole.

So many things could be written with profit on the study of words, but let us briefly note some comments on the importance of some seemingly little words.

In your Bible study watch for verbs of command, and then look for the teaching, either before or after them, that explains or supports them. Alertness to this will profit you greatly. The four "I haves" and six "I wills" given earlier, when dealing with verse study, illustrate the point.

Observation of connectives will help you to establish relationships—to find how a sentence or a paragraph is linked to what precedes it or follows it. Note two kinds of connectives:

1. Logical connectives that indicate various relationships.

2. Emphatic connectives that indicate various emphases.

CONNECTIVES OF LOGIC

Connectives of reason explain why a statement is true. They appear either before or after the statement with which they deal. Common among these are "since," "because," "for," "if." Follow these in Romans 1. Verses 16-21 illustrate the point.

Connectives of result illustrate how one truth gives the reasons for another. Examples are "then," "so," "therefore," "wherefore." See Romans 9:15, 16 and Galatians 2:21. *Whenever you find a "therefore" find out what it's there for.* Compare Romans 5:1; 8:1; 12:1.

Connectives of purpose state the result to be obtained. Examples are "so that" (1 Corinthians 1:6, 7) and "to the end" (Romans 4:16).

Connectives of contrast explain how two ideas differ. Among these are the commonly used term "but" (Romans 2:2-11; 3:21; 5:8; 10:6). A beautiful expression of contrast, "much more," appears in a series in Romans 5:9, 10, 17, 20. These terms occur in many other passages. Some others are "although" (Mark 14: 29); "yet" (1 Corinthians 5:10); "else" (1 Corinthians 14:16); "nevertheless" (1 Corinthians 9:12).

Connectives of comparison indicate how two truths are alike. Common among these are "likewise" (Romans 6:11); "also" (2 Corinthians 1:21, 22); "as" and "so" (Romans 12:4, 5; 5:18; 11:30, 31); "as" (Romans 9:25); "so likewise" (1 Corinthians 14:9; Luke 17:10); "even as" (Romans 4:6).

Connectives of series bring a number of ideas, events, or facts together. In 1 Timothy 2:1 we find one such term, "first of all." First Corinthians 15:8 gives another, "last of all." Second Corinthians 6:14-16 gives a series which might also be termed contrasts.

CONNECTIVES OF EMPHASIS

Emphatic connectives set forth important points. Note these: "indeed" (Romans 14:20); "only" (Romans 4:9, 12; 5:3, 11; 8:23).

The importance of these words is not so much in their meaning as in the relationships they convey. Be alert to them. They will enrich truth to you.

EXAMPLE OF CONNECTIVES

The following study (pages 115, 116), taken from 1 Corinthians 2, is a good illustration of how connectives are used to bring sharp contrast. In this case the wisdom of man is contrasted with the wisdom of God.

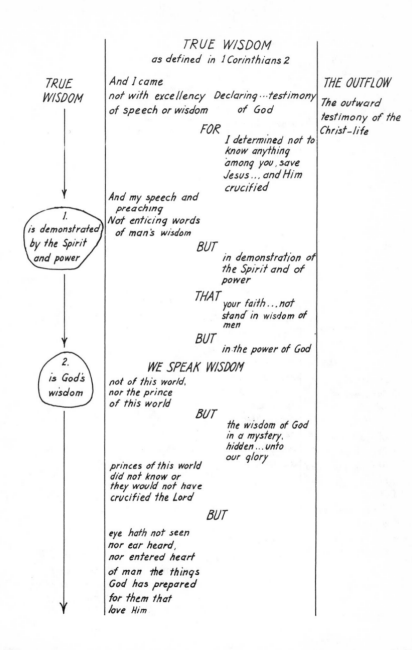

TRUE WISDOM
as defined in 1 Corinthians 2

TRUE
WISDOM

And I came
not with excellency Declaring···testimony
of speech or wisdom   of God

FOR

I determined not to
know anything
among you, save
Jesus...and Him
crucified

And my speech and
preaching
Not enticing words
of man's wisdom

BUT

in demonstration of
the Spirit and of
power

THAT

your faith...not
stand in wisdom of
men

BUT

in the power of God

WE SPEAK WISDOM

not of this world,
nor the prince
of this world

BUT

the wisdom of God
in a mystery,
hidden...unto
our glory

princes of this world
did not know or
they would not have
crucified the Lord

BUT

eye hath not seen
nor ear heard,
nor entered heart

of man the things
God has prepared
for them that
love Him

1.
is demonstrated
by the Spirit
and power

2.
is God's
wisdom

THE OUTFLOW

The outward
testimony of the
Christ-life

3.
is received by the Spirit

TRUE WISDOM KNOWS

1. Christ and Him crucified
2. The power of the Holy Spirit
3. The hidden things of God
4. The things God has prepared for us
5. The things freely given us of God
6. The mind of Christ

BUT
    God hath revealed them unto us by the Spirit
      for the Spirit searcheth all things, yea, the deep things

What man knoweth ...the things of God knoweth no man

BUT
    the Spirit knoweth

NOW
we have received not the spirit of the world

BUT   of Christ

THAT
    we might know the things freely given to us of God

BUT
the natural man receiveth not the things of God... foolishness unto him : neither can he know...they are spiritually discerned

BUT
    he that is spiritual judgeth all things

FOR
Who hath known the mind of the Lord

BUT
    we have the mind of Christ

THE INFLOW
The inward resource of the Christ-mind

11

Teaching the Scriptures

THE RESPONSIBILITY AND PRIVILEGE of teaching the Bible, usually within the curriculum of the Sunday school, is given to thousands of Christians. Bible teaching, when backed by adequate preparation and undergirded with prayer, is a thrilling experience. This channel of service can provide rewards that will last for all eternity.

Bible teaching must be done by those who know the Bible and believe it. This will make for an authority on the part of the teacher which will be recognized by the student. This authority is threefold:

1. That which comes from the Bible itself. It is, "Thus saith the Lord."

2. That which Jesus revealed. He accepted the Scriptures for what they are—God speaking to men.

3. That which comes by the Holy Spirit. He leads us into all truth and enables us to understand it, and equips us to teach it.

Effective teaching requires discipline on the part of the teacher. It will be reflected in the time blocks set aside for study and preparation. Good preparation and successful teaching hinge on goals or objectives, both long-range and short-range. Continual attention must be given to sharpening skills. Soul preparation is of vital importance.

P. G. Wade has set forth the following as the

SEVEN LAWS OF SUCCESSFUL TEACHING

1. Law of the teacher: The teacher must know that which he would teach.

2. Law of the pupil: The pupil must attend with interest to the material being taught.

3. Law of the language: The language used in teaching must be common to both teacher and pupil.

4. Law of the lesson: The truth to be taught must be learned through truth already known.

5. Law of the teaching process: The teacher must excite and direct the self-activities of the pupil.

6. Law of the learning process: The pupil must reproduce in his own mind the truths to be learned.

7. Law of review and application: The completion, test, and confirmation of the work of teaching must be made by review and application.

LESSON PREPARATION

You, the teacher, are the lesson you teach. Let that fact strike home and you will never be careless about lesson preparation.

Your lesson is taken from one of the 66 books of the Bible. Can you shut your eyes and picture its contents? How clear in your mind is the thread of argument in the short passage on which today's lesson is based?

There are two kinds of preparation. First, the general background accumulation of lesson content, teaching technique, and practical psychology. This is assimilated over a long period of time. Second, the specific effort for a particular session dealing with a particular subject and a particular class.

There are two focal planes of teaching. First, there is the lesson content itself. Second, there is the pupil. Never forget, you are not teaching lessons; you are teaching persons!

For this reason, preparation comes in two parts. First, there is preparation to teach the lesson. Second, there is preparation to teach the lesson to pupils. This simple acrostic outlines preparation:

P ray
R ead the Bible
E nrich background
P repare materials and room
A im lesson
R elate to the student
E valuate

Aiming the Lesson

Teaching a lesson without a specific aim is like shooting a gun without having a target. "He who aims at nothing is sure to hit it."

Ask yourself some questions. What is there in this lesson to appeal to the intellect of the students, the emotions of the students, the will of the students? What do I want them to know? What do I want them to feel? What do I want them to do?

A lesson plan will keep the teacher pointed toward a goal and will guarantee that his material is organized and that the lesson will be covered. It will insure relevancy and will relate each lesson to the unit objective. With no goal in mind, the teacher wastes time on nonessentials, and his teaching is too often unrelated to the life needs of the students.

It is generally agreed that successful lesson planning will involve three objectives: (1) to teach knowledge, (2) to bring inspiration, (3) to bring about conduct response. Normally a lesson will be planned with only one of these aims in mind, or at least only one will be dominant.

If the purpose of a lesson is to communicate Biblical information, the teacher will plan the lesson with a knowledge or content aim. If the purpose is to touch the emotions, to inspire, the lesson will have an inspiration aim. While this is a response aim, there is a more specific aim for conduct response. If teachers are to secure results in the Christian maturity of their students, the conduct response must be dominant, and the aim must be very specific. As the teacher plans the lesson he must think in terms of the learner response he hopes to attain.

Teaching for Conduct Response

No curriculum writer can hope to prepare materials that will meet the specific needs of a given class. But he patterns a series of lessons with a series of helps to assist the teacher. After the writer has done his work, the rest is up to the teacher. No teacher should expect a lesson to be effective until he has first made it effective to himself.

Next, the teacher will want to prayerfully aim the lesson to the needs of his students. First, he will want to help the students see the facts of the passage clearly. Second, he will want to help the students understand what it means. Third, the teacher will want to help the students know how to apply the lesson in their own lives.

In other words, the teacher wants the students to know the facts, feel the principles, and make the applications. The appeal is to the intellect, the emotions, and the will, moving from the head to the heart to the hand. Until the teacher knows where he wants to take his students, he cannot expect to be effective.

Structuring the Lesson Plan

Regardless of the format of the lesson plan, a good lesson has a four-step pattern, as pointed out by Lawrence O. Richards.[1] Richards defines these as hook, Book, look, and took.

The purpose of a lesson hook is to get attention. It can also set the goal. Gaining the attention of the students from the start of the session is extremely important. One way to do this is to begin with an anecdote, either humorous or serious. A startling question can be an effective attention-getter. But if such a question is to attract sharp minds it must be thought-provoking. Questions most likely to draw discussion are "why" and "how" questions.

An effective hook must always flow effectively into the Book. This step is for the purpose of presenting the Biblical information and helping the students to understand it.

The next step is the look. This is the process whereby the teacher relates the passage to life. Effective teaching will show the students what they should do and how they should respond.

There are several guidelines to keep in focus when applying Bible truths. First, the application must relate to the student's life and not the teacher's. Second, it should parallel the truth of the lesson. Third, make it specific. Fourth, relate the application to areas of struggle in the lives of the students. Fifth, make it motivate the students to respond to God. Sixth, let it be unhurried.

[1] *Creative Bible Teaching* (Chicago: Moody Press, 1970).

The final step in structuring the lesson is the took. This means that it "takes"; that it brings response. One teacher held his class of boys spellbound with the story of the problems, perils, and promotions of Joseph. As a story it was told perfectly; but when the story was over, it was over. He failed to attempt application.

Another teacher told the same story, giving greater understanding by showing how it pictured the suffering and death of Christ and His final coronation as King of kings and Lord of lords.

A third teacher told the story, related it to Christ, but went one step further by getting himself and the boys personally involved and causing them to make a decision. God's Word is not given to us so that we can recite back the facts. It demands action.

DETERMINING THE METHOD

Good teaching depends on the teacher understanding his aim and desiring to get it across. In that sense teaching methods are incidental. There are many methods to be used, and they can all be used at one time or another with great profit. Excellent material can be studied on the advantages and disadvantages of the lecture method, the narrative, the recitation, the question and answer method, the discussion, the project, and the handwork method. Buzz sessions and panels can also be effective.

Jesus used varied techniques. He used illustrations to brighten things up and let in light. He used questions and answers to stimulate thought, clarify thinking, and bring His listeners to conclusions. By exposure He turned the searchlight of His wisdom on the value judgments of His hearers.

A LESSON PLAN

1. Aim for the quarter
2. Lesson aim
3. Securing attention and interest
4. Transition to the Scripture passage
5. Developing the lesson

6. Making the lesson personal
7. Securing the response

PLANNING A SPECIFIC LESSON

Let us highlight a lesson from John 11, dealing with the death and resurrection of Lazarus.

The teacher will ask himself several questions when preparing the lesson plan. What are the needs of my class? Are some unsaved? Lukewarm in their spiritual experience? Are members facing serious problems? In sorrow? In need of hope? Of cheer? The answers will determine the aim. Shall it be a knowledge response? An inspiration response? A conduct response? What kind of conduct response?

A hook could be drawn from many life situations. Let us use one from the ministry of Pastor H. W. Barber, of Calvary Temple, Winnipeg, Manitoba. For the sake of brevity, some essential details must be omitted.

The pastor was called to a hospital following a terrible car accident to find a young bride in serious condition. To her anxious question concerning her husband, the attending doctor had to respond, "I'm sorry, he's dead." She seemed to pass into shock, and the doctor had to leave while the pastor remained.

Suddenly she cried out, "Where is he now?" After ascertaining that she was coherent, the pastor tried to assure her of God's love and wisdom. But then she said both of them had once been Christians, and just days before they agreed they must come back to God. Again the pastor attempted to give her a ray of hope, but she responded by saying that they and the other passengers were drinking in the car on their way to the big football game when the tragedy occurred. "Where is he now?"

Death is always cold and has been feared throughout the ages. According to Hebrews 2:15, in the days of the apostles people lived in fear of death. It was thought of as a prison with the gates closing forever.

It appears from Paul's letters to the Thessalonians that they had gotten an excellent grasp of doctrine in the brief time since their conversion from heathenism. He taught them the doctrine of the Second Coming in the "three sabbaths" spent with them (Acts 17). They believed it so much that they didn't expect to die, but death came to their members. Apparently the Thessalonians in their ignorance (1 Thessalonians 4:13-18) believed that the living would be taken and the dead left at the Lord's coming. In his letter to them Paul gives the great truth of the resurrection.

In John 11 Jesus taught and illustrated the truth of resurrection. He performed the miracle to support His claim to divinity as being the "resurrection, and the life" (John 11:25). Refer to the inductive method of studying this text as given in chapter 7. Develop your observation and interpretation, and then make the needed application.

The application could be one of several. It might call for decision for Christ to be ready for our time of departure from this life; or the assurance and comfort to those who have walked the road of sorrow; or the need of making the choice of Mary rather than of the practical Martha who was "cumbered about much serving" (Luke 10:38-42; John 12:1-9); or the concern and compassion of a loving Lord who is "touched with the feeling of our infirmities" (Hebrews 4:14-16).

Consider the closing prayer time. If the students have learned and felt the truth of God's Word, they need to be encouraged to apply it in real-life situations. To this end, prayer with them is vital.

PREPARING TO TEACH CHILDREN

The principles set forth in this chapter are applicable to teaching any age-group. The important thing is to make the lesson relevant to the comprehension of the age-group being taught. The balance of the chapter will be devoted specifically to teaching children.

The needs of children are very real; needs are not restricted to adults alone. And God does have a message for children in His Word.

Let us look at some factors that today affect the learning abilities of children. First, today's world has changed children rapidly. They are more urbanized and more transient. Mobility has taken them to many places and possibly a number of schools. They have watched thousands of hours of television. Their world and life image is totally different than that which their parents had at that age. Second, more can be expected of them. Third, learning can be an enjoyable experience.

Further, there are the age-old problems children face which have greatly increased in recent years. We refer to the effects of alcohol, drugs, broken homes, adjustments to a new parent in a divorce-remarriage situation, and other complexities of life today. Unless the teacher knows his or her pupils and their home problems, he or she will be teaching children as groups instead of as individuals with personal needs.

With these factors in mind, the teacher will keep certain basics in clear focus. First, the lesson must be made relevant to the present needs of the children. Second, the truth taught must be faithful to the Scriptures. The Bible teaches more than morals and good works; the child can experience a personal relation with God. Third, the Bible must be applied to the child's level of comprehension.

This means that lessons should be structured so as to lead children to make their own decisions and responses to the Lord in a meaningful way. Children should know the Lord's Prayer, the Twenty-third Psalm, and similar Scripture passages. But these should not become a rote substitute for a personal comprehension and experience in the life of the child. This is said with a clear belief, however, that the child who grows up absorbing Bible stories will receive great profit. Our plea is for careful guidance in the teaching ministry so that the greatest spiritual results will be obtained.

"There are two primary requirements for Bible study," states Lawrence Richards, "that will best help children understand what God has to say to them. The first is being sure that what we teach is actually what God is saying. The second is creative structuring of the teaching-learning situation."

The final goal of our work is spiritual. The true teacher is an evangelist. He is not merely content to teach about God; he strives to help his students to know God. Thus his work centers in the pupil's personal decision to accept Christ as Saviour and to live as God's child.

The natural time for decision is in adolescence. The awakening of interest in and the decision to love and serve God are natural aspects of the general expansion of selfhood in the adolescent. Decision for Christ should not be forced, but every effort should be made to see that decision is made before life has begun to acquire its set.

The teacher will need to guard against the student's making his decision on the basis of the teacher's authority. If the teacher makes the application of the truth, his authority may be substituted for that of the truth itself. The ultimate decision must be on the authority of the pure gold of truth if it is to be lasting.

Teachers of children must point them to right choices and must put the map of God's Word in their hands to guide them along life's journey. Use all the modern means of conveying the message to their hearts. Talk to them on their level and illustrate the lesson with things from everyday life.

A subject or activity becomes interesting when it gives one an opportunity to express his ideas. Therefore, teaching that creates interest is that which appeals to the student's own ideas. To accomplish this the teacher makes the pupil understand the truth and welcome it. The teacher will get the student's viewpoint and see the truth through his eyes. It has been said that the successful preacher is able to stand in the pulpit and metaphorically sit in the pew at the same time. This truth applies to the teacher, too. He looks through his students' eyes and presents his lesson against their backgrounds.

Jesus presented His truths from His listener's viewpoint. He came teaching the deepest truths concerning God, man, and human existence. He made His teaching clear to simple, unlettered people by telling them that the kingdom of God was like some things they already understood: "the kingdom of heaven is likened unto a man which sowed . . . a grain of mustard seed . . . leaven . . . treasure . . . man seeking pearls . . . a net" (Matthew 13). Notice how Jesus called Andrew, Peter, James, and John. He didn't couch the call in theological terms. They were fishermen, and He called them, saying, "Follow me and I will make you fishers of men."

When the teacher appeals to the students' ideas, he wins their interest; if he gains their interest, he can hold their attention; and if he holds their attention, he will be able to impart the truth of the lesson. Let us look at a few ways of gaining and holding attention.

USING THE CHALKBOARD

The chalkboard can be used to outline the lesson, to draw illustrating pictures, to paraphrase the Scripture passage, to teach the memory verse, to write down the answers and ideas of the students, to make assignments, to define words, to review lessons.

The ingenious teacher automatically captures attention when he takes a piece of chalk in his hand. Use that piece of chalk even if you are not an expert at sketching or drawing. Children are great at imagining, and they will visualize what you draw as you relate the picture.

USING OTHER VISUALS

There are numerous methods of visual and audio instruction available to teachers. Inexpensive materials can be used effectively. One picture is still worth a thousand words. Both children and adults remember what they see.

You can teach by the sense of sight through pictures, filmstrips, chalkboard, and many other eyegate methods. Learning can come by the sense of sound through the use of a trumpet in connection with a lesson on Joshua's march around Jericho. Or the children could explore the sense of touch by the use of a twig of thorns to illustrate Jesus' crown of thorns, or bringing a locust to illustrate the food of John the Baptist. A bouquet of flowers can be used to illustrate the Rose of Sharon, the Lily of the Valley, the fragrance of the Christ-life, or of praise and prayer ascending to God. In like manner, truth can be illustrated through the sense of taste.

USING QUESTIONS

Never forget that the question the student asks is more important than the questions the teacher asks. The unexpected and irrelevant question never troubled the Lord. He was always able to turn an interruption into an advantage; He made it point out the road He was going to take. Luke 12 records that Jesus was interrupted in the midst of a teaching session by an irrelevant question from a lawyer. It is possible that we might not have had the lesson on covetousness and the parable about the wealthy farmer had Jesus not been disturbed by an irrelevant question (v. 13). Often questions arise from momentary interests. Let such a question be your guide even though it may take you on a circuitous route to your ultimate destination. It's better to get the questioner along with you than to turn him off.

The proper use of questions by a teacher is of the utmost importance. Teachers should ask one specific thing at a time, and questions should be brief, clear, and definite. They should be asked to stimulate real thought and be arranged in logical order so that each grows out of what has gone before, and leads up to what is to follow, thus unfolding the topic. Ask questions conversationally, naturally, informally. Ask them of the whole class, then call on an individual. Don't always call on the bright students, the same ones, nor on pupils in consecutive order. Allow students time to think through and formulate answers. If a student's answer is incomplete, encourage him to think further. Asking questions is an art every teacher should cultivate and learn to use with the greatest possible skill.

STORYTELLING

A story gains immediate attention. The story used should be well told and be well chosen to accomplish the needed purpose. Note the following points regarding this important teaching device:

1. *Beginning:* Let it be brief and attention-getting immediately. The atmosphere is set, and at least the leading characters are

introduced. The central conflict—a part of stories—is presented. Use strong, descriptive verbs and modifiers.

2. *Body:* Action moves from the introduction and continues from incident to incident, picture to picture. Every part must contribute to solving the central conflict: evil versus good, Satan against God, darkness against light. Each incident creates suspense building to the

3. *Climax:* Suspense has spent its force, and at this point interest diminishes rapidly. The story is over, and the summary must be brief.

4. *Conclusion:* This is of vital importance. Let it be thought out clearly so that the hearers will make the proper response.

5. *General observations:* Follow only one thread of thought even though the story may have two or three. Explain the unknown in terms of the known. Do not let the story degenerate into mere entertainment, nor allow storytelling to divert general teaching which would require more independent thinking. Above all, never read your story.

CONCLUSION

The Sunday school teacher must keep up on new ways to apply the truth. Some methods work well with children, but not with young people and adults, and vice versa. The teacher's task is to utilize whatever he can to accomplish the greatest project ever given to men—the application of eternal truth to the lives of eternal souls.

Seek for ways to put Bible truths on the level of your class. You may think that, because you are teaching small children, you don't need as much ability and wisdom as the adult teacher. But all teachers need prayerful preparation and divine anointing.

Learning best takes place when the learner has opportunity to express himself, and commit himself to the principles taught. Expression in the class enables the teacher to identify wrong patterns of thinking. And remember the essence of the educative process: a teacher can tell a student something, but the student must see it, must experience it for himself, before the knowledge is truly his.